Copyright © 2018 by Kei LUBUSA

All rights reserved. No part of this book may be reproduced or transmitted in any form or by any means, electronic or mechanical, including photocopying, recording, or by any information storage and retrieval system, without the written permission of the Publisher, except where permitted by law.

Coloring Book

For adults

30 relaxing Mandala

ISBN-13: 9781790295036

FREE DOWNLOAD BONUS

+5 Mandala in PDF file

Website:
www.SMARTGORILLABOOKS.com

Code : "MANDALA40"

A Special request :
Your brief Amazon review could really help us.

You're free to leave a comment at this page:
www.SmartGorillaBooks.com/mandala

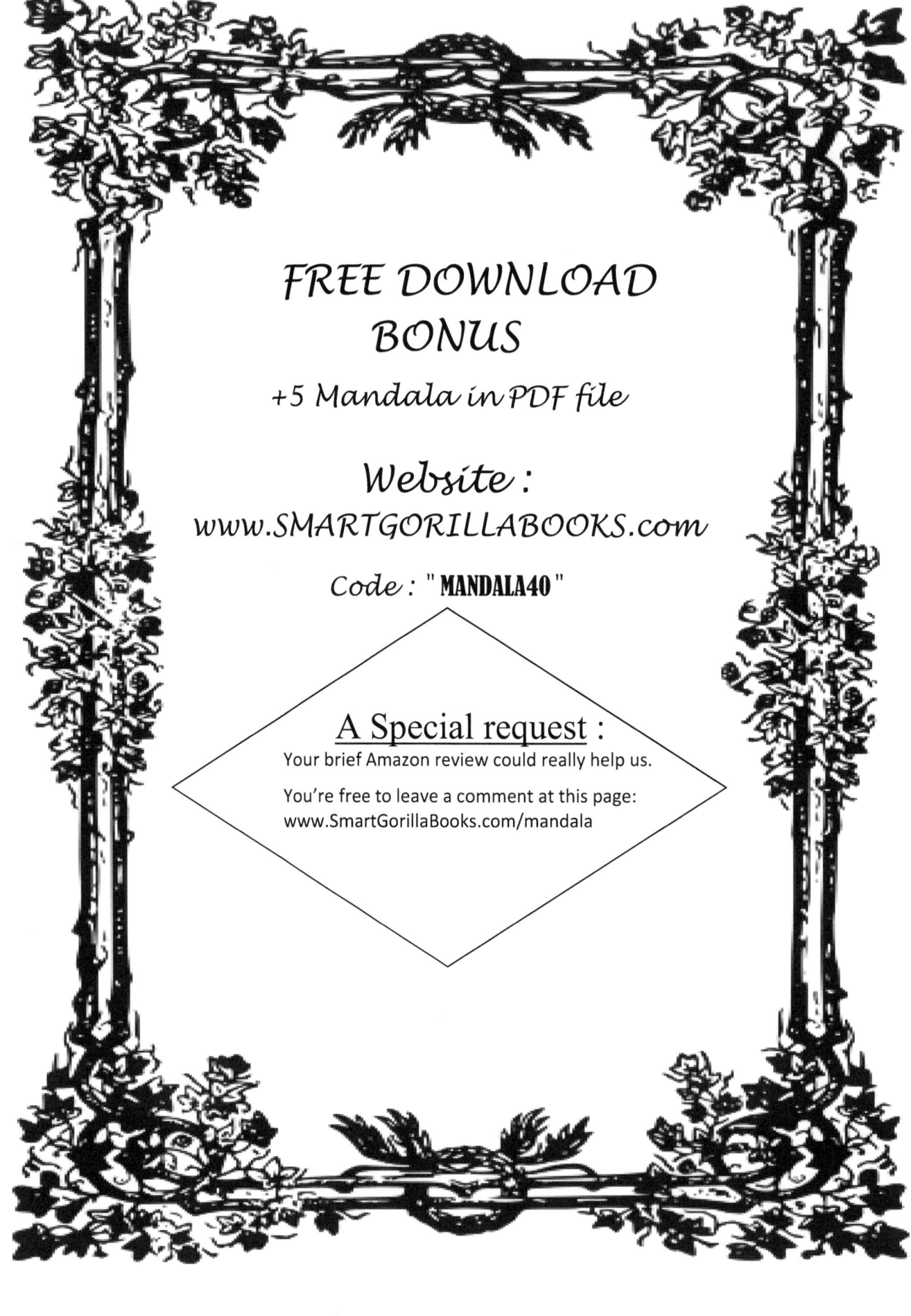

30 beautiful mandala designed by an artist

This book is the perfect way for beginner colorists to create beautiful and colorful mandala.

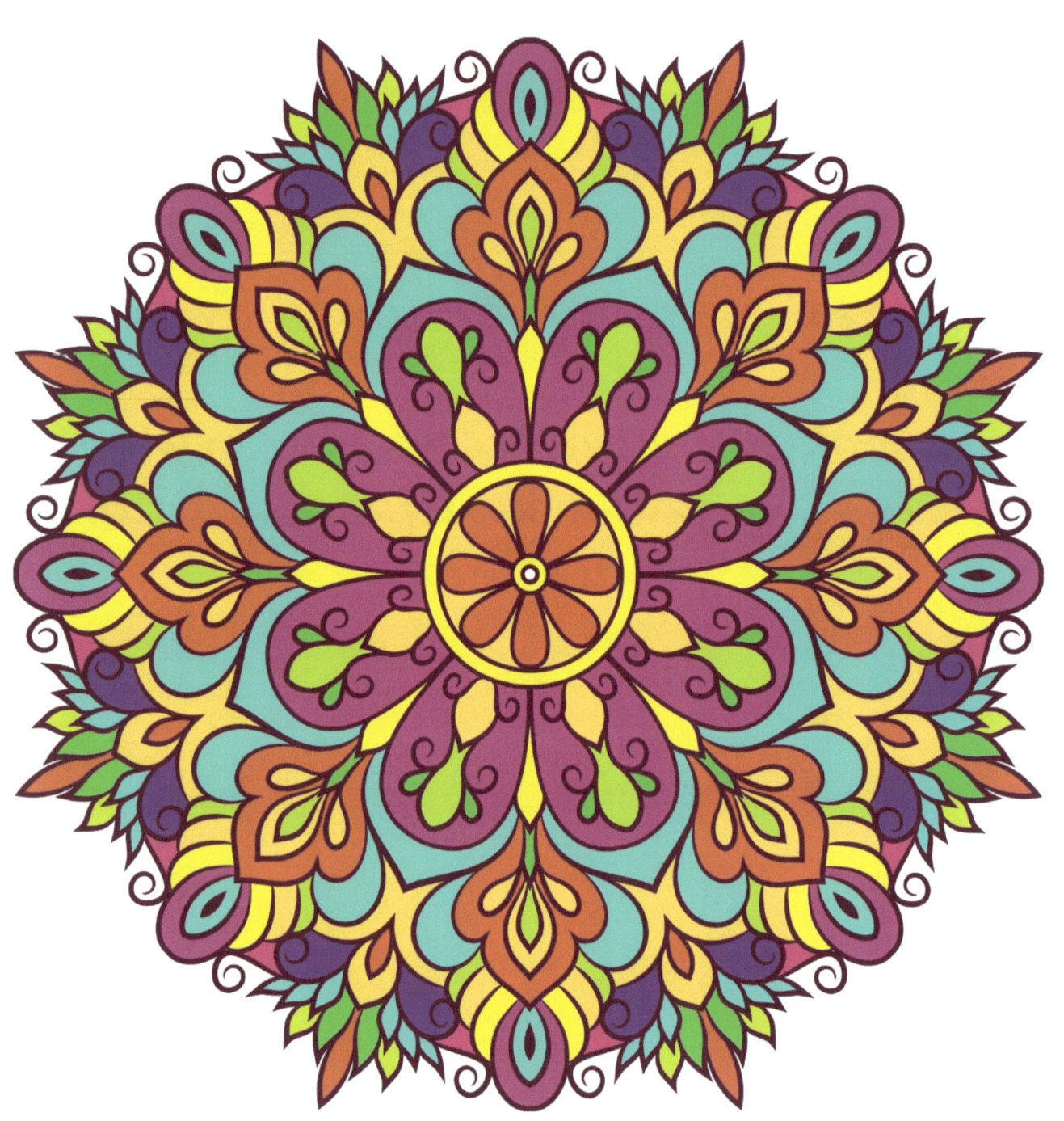

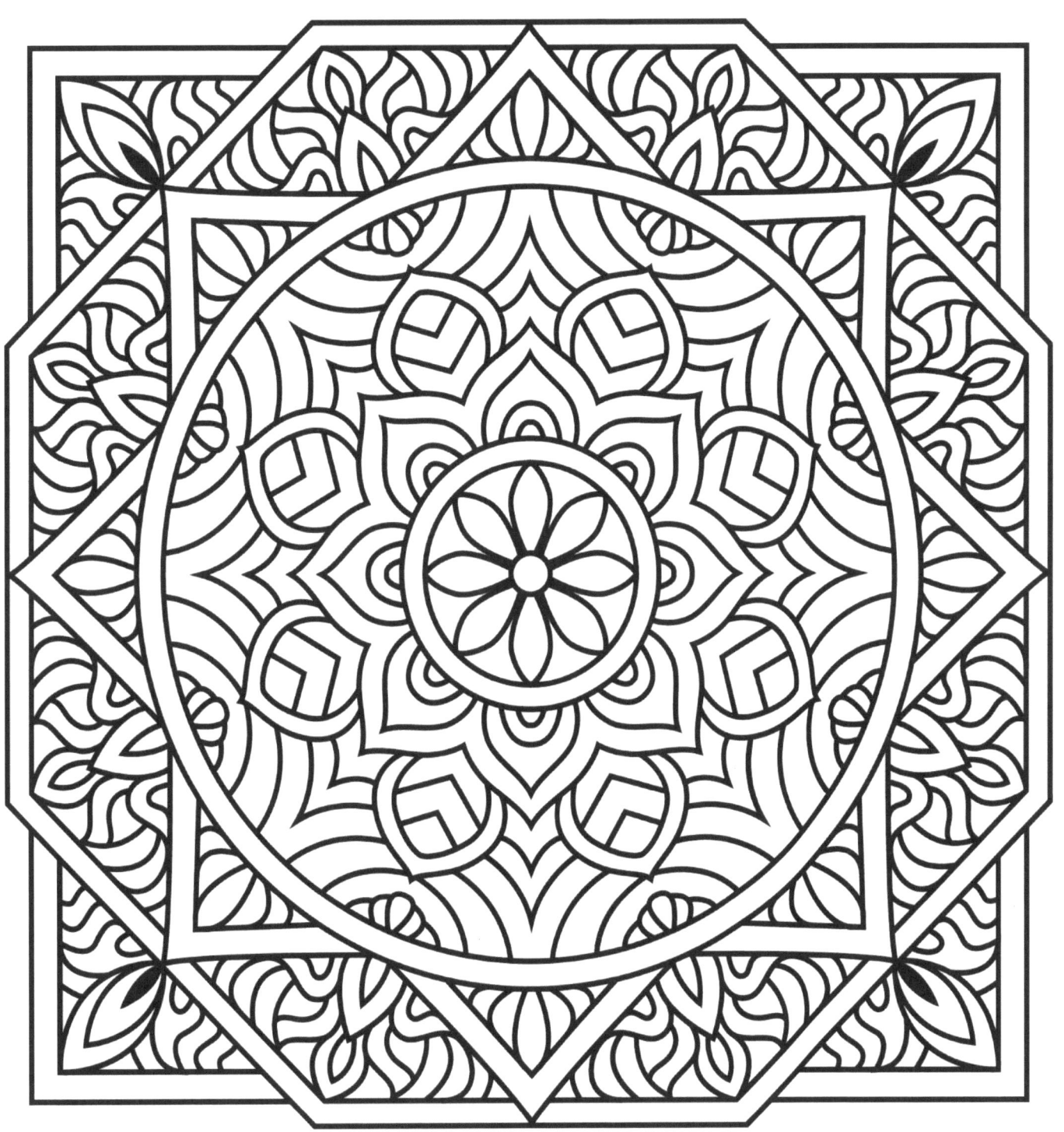

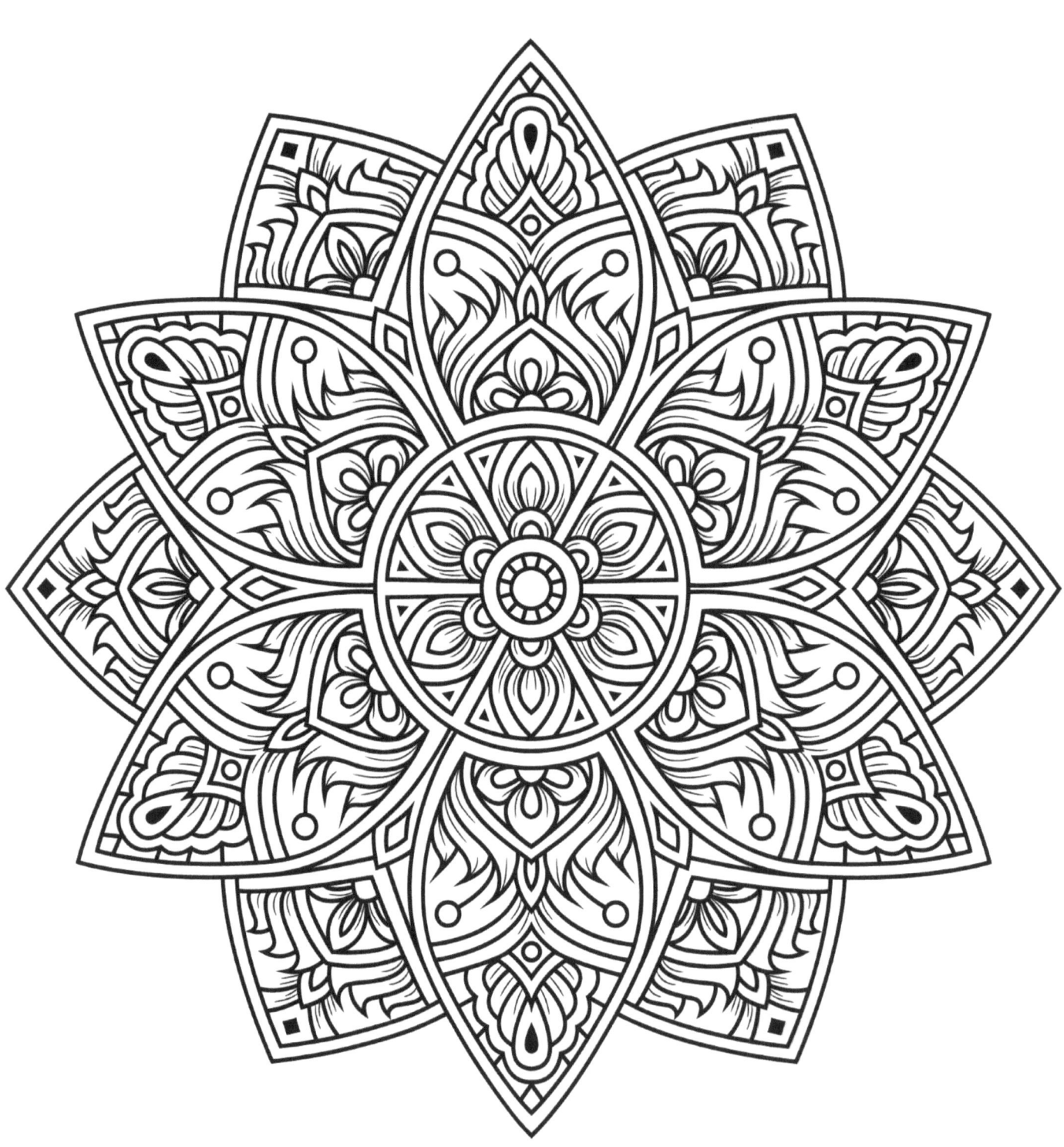

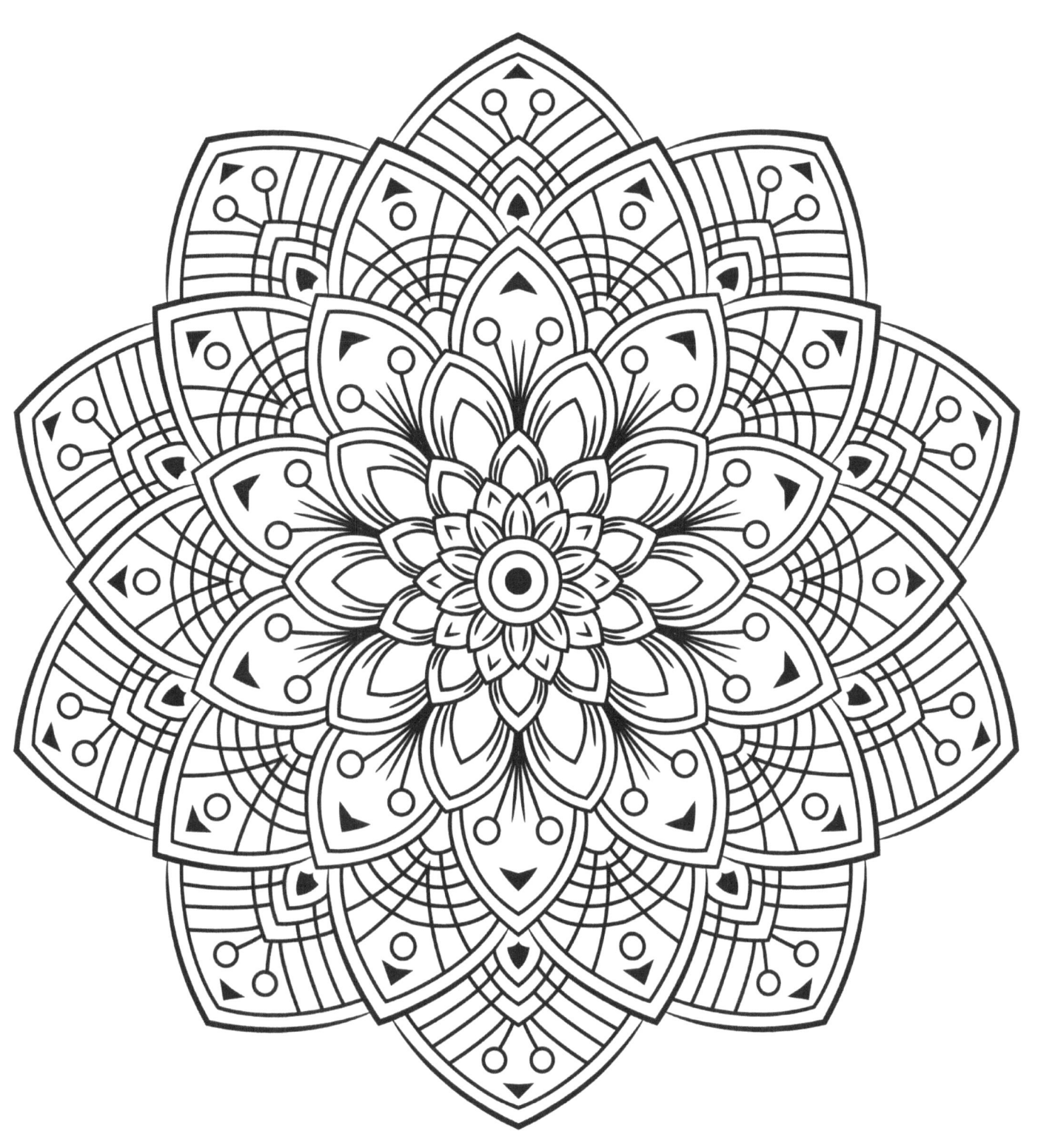

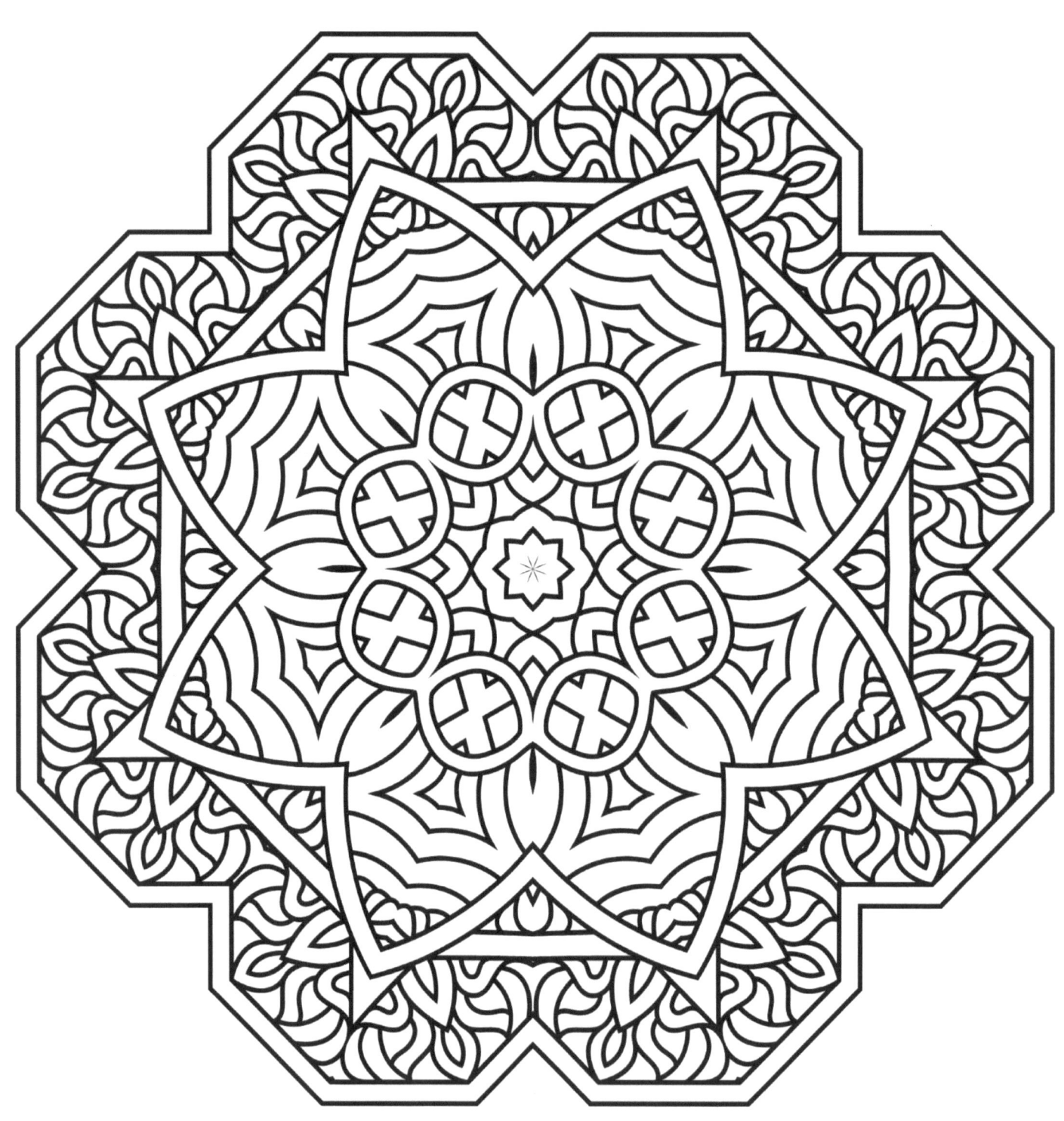

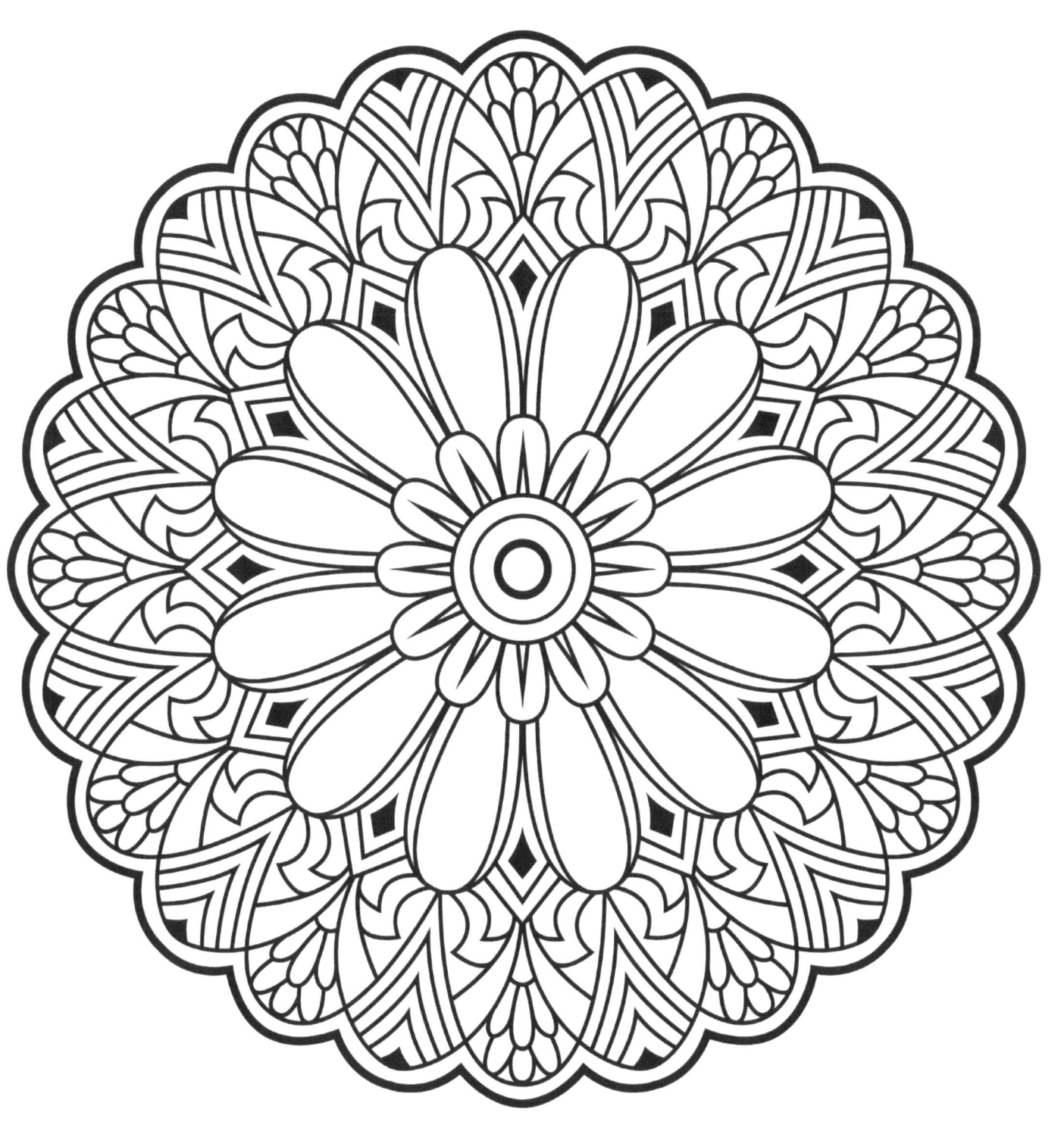

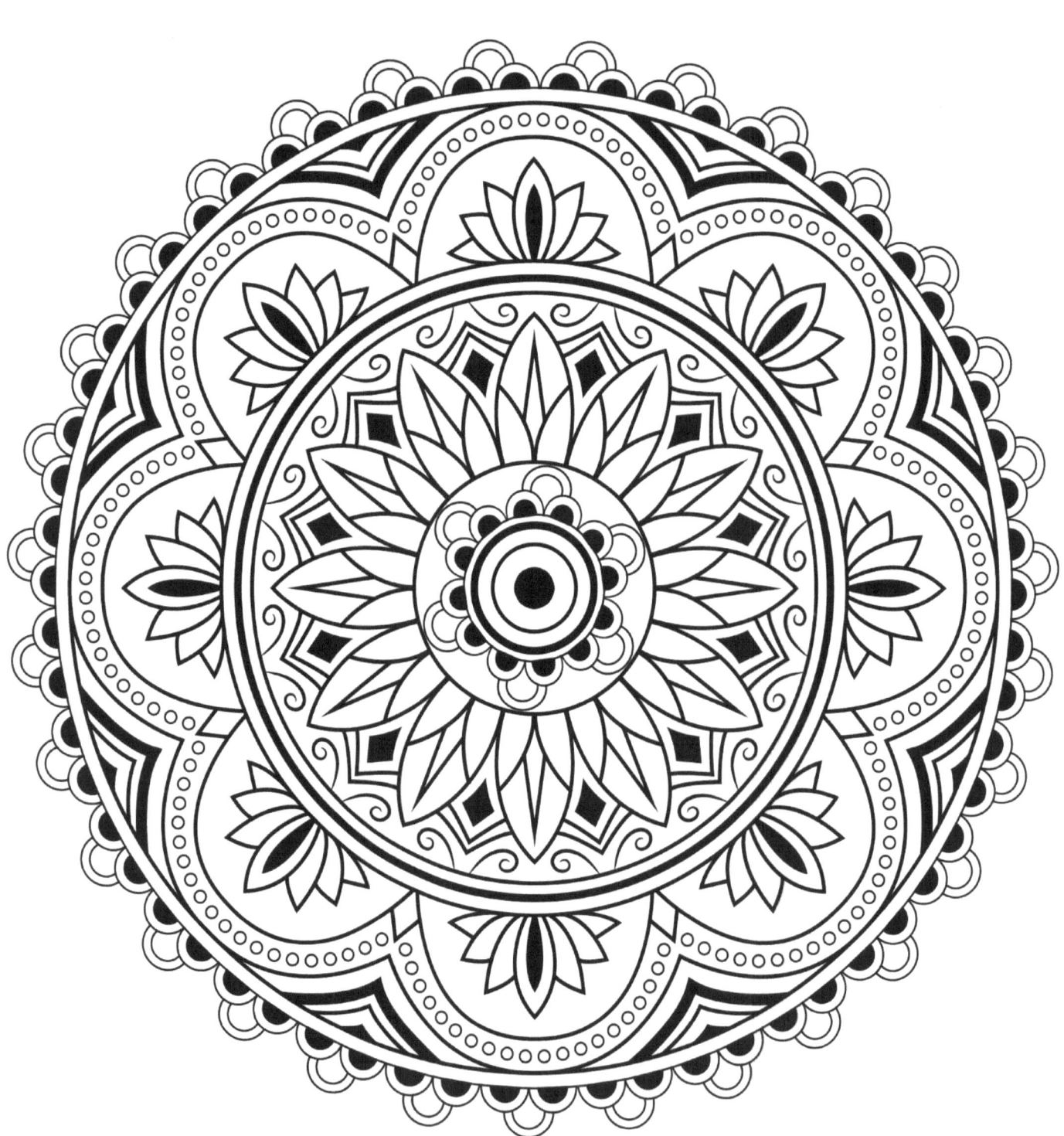

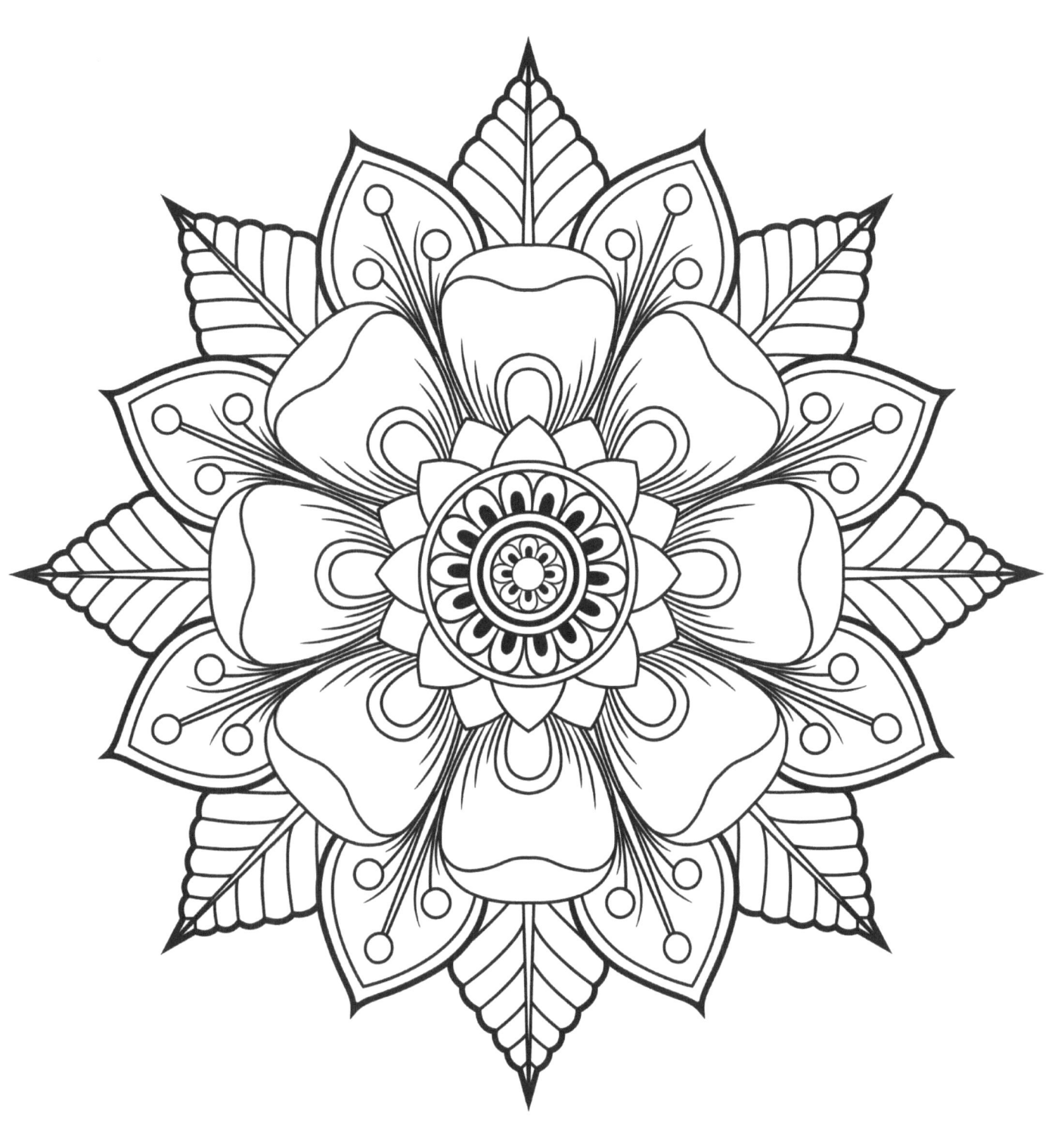

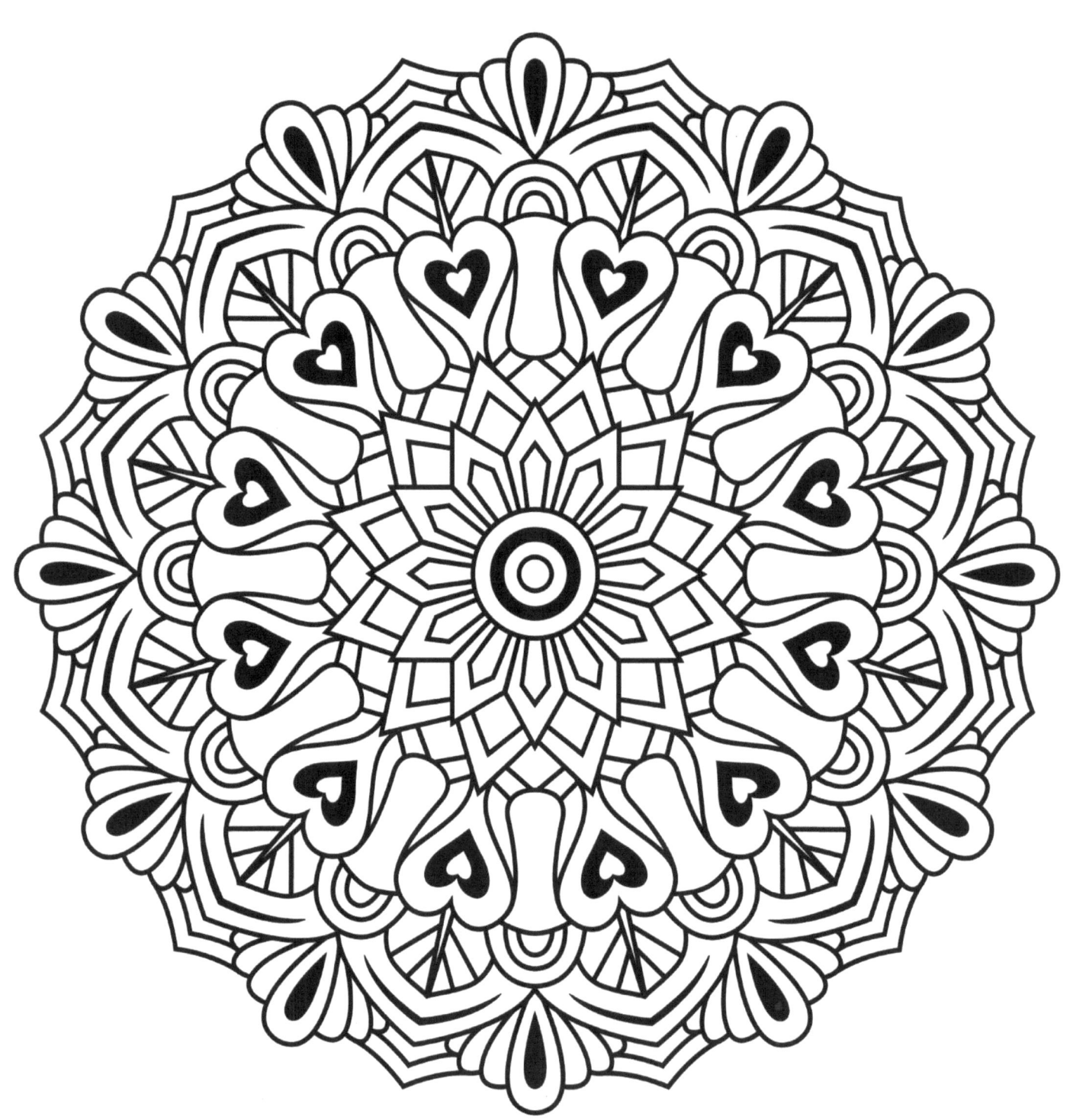

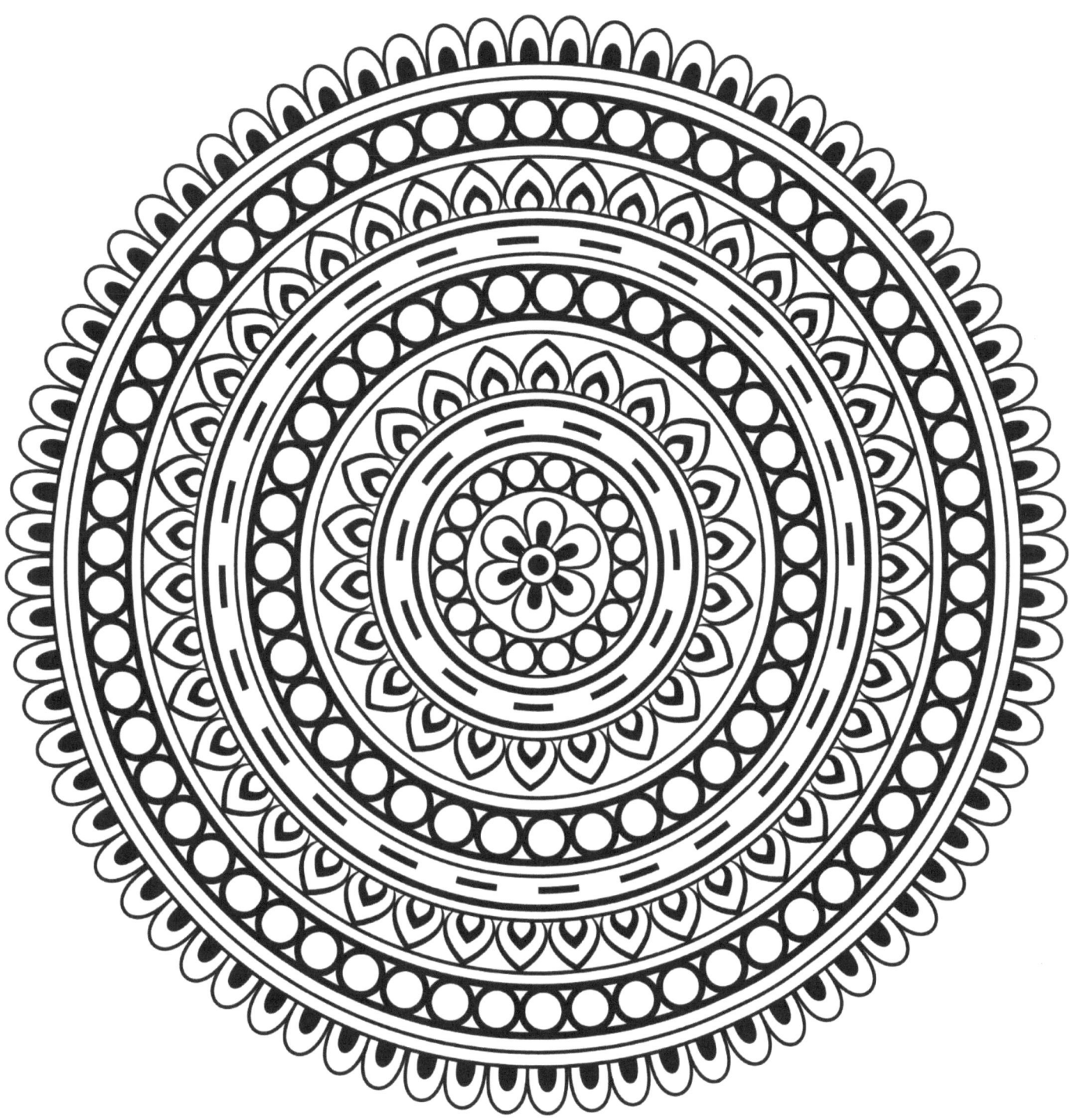

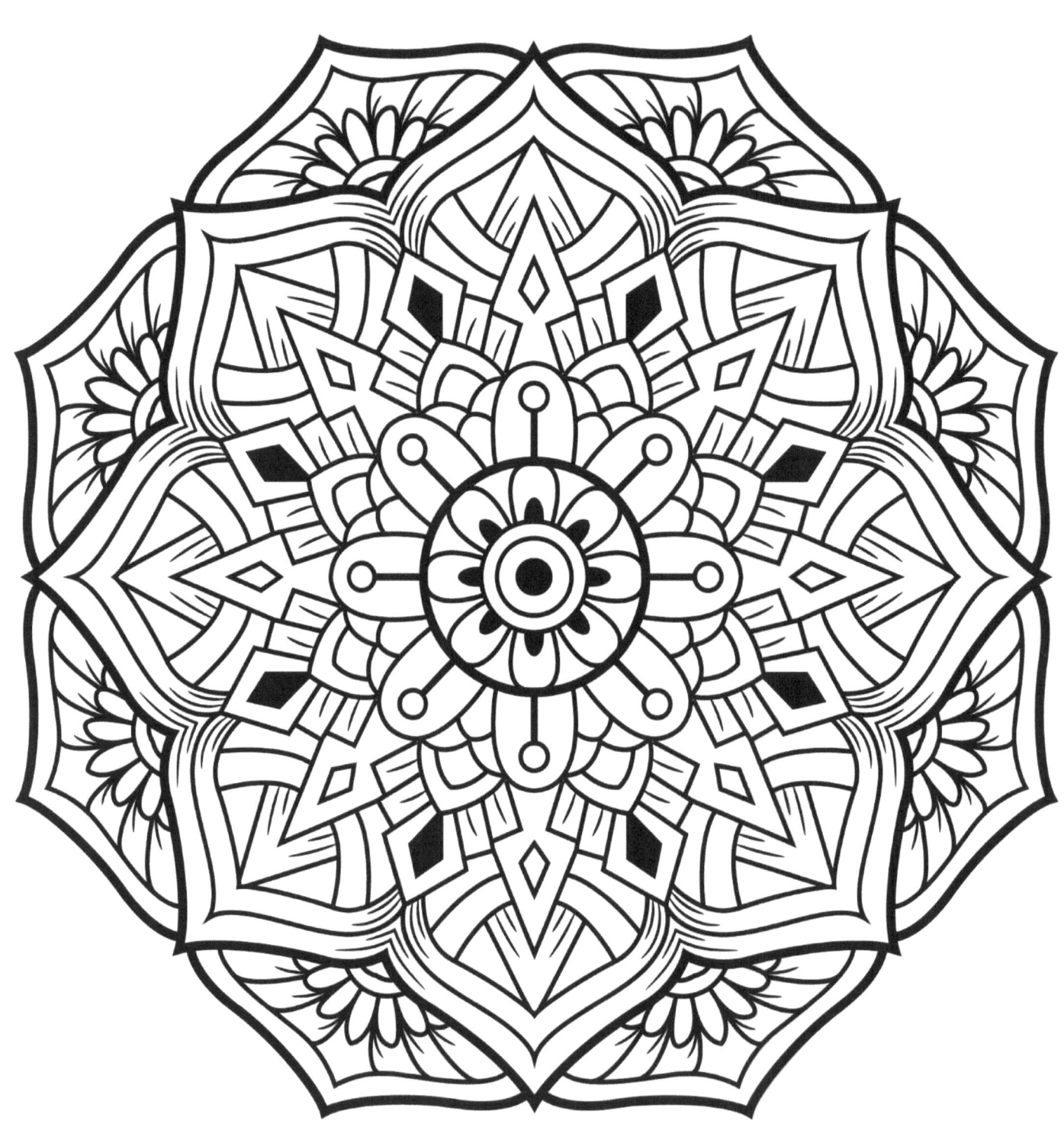

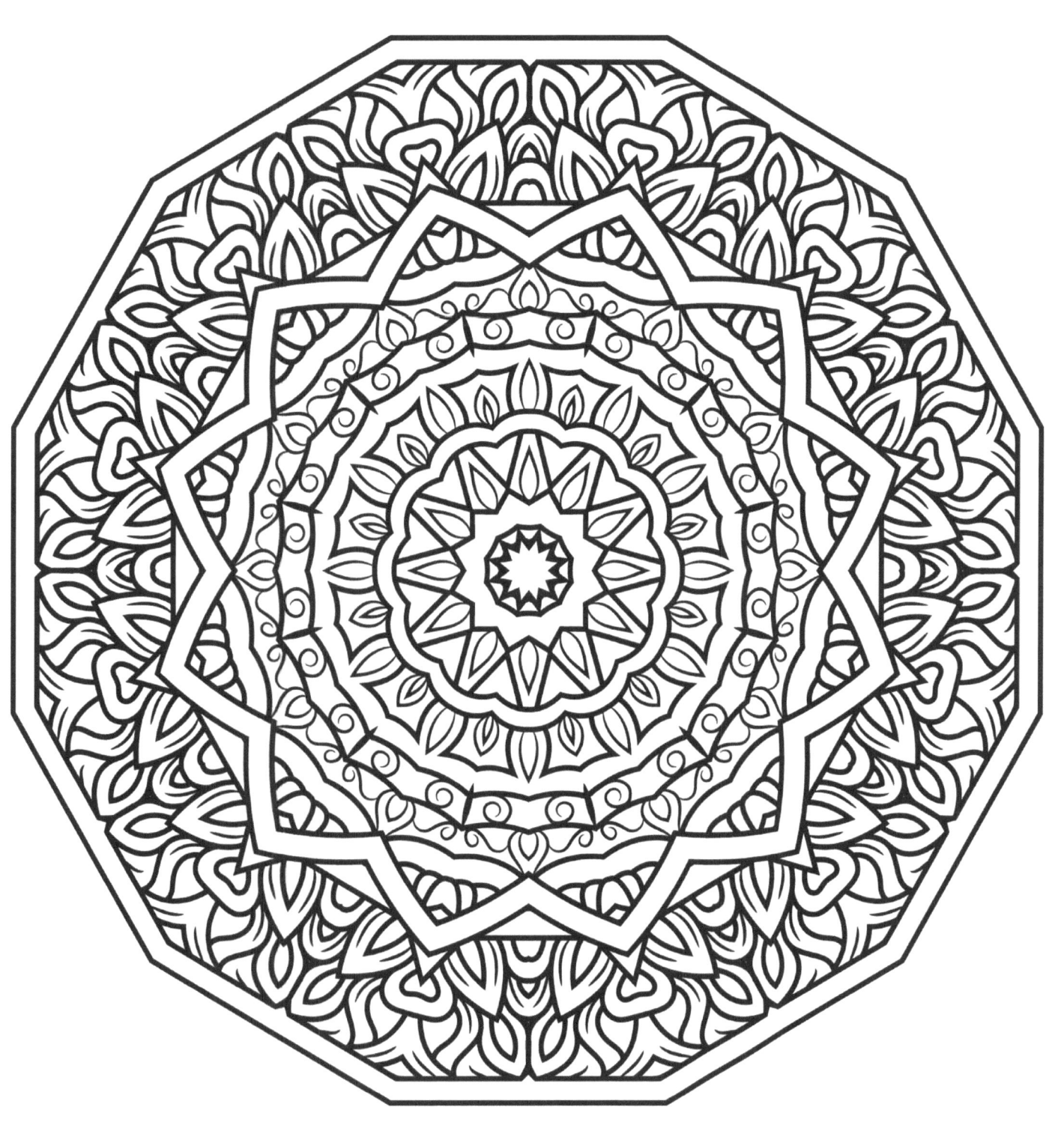

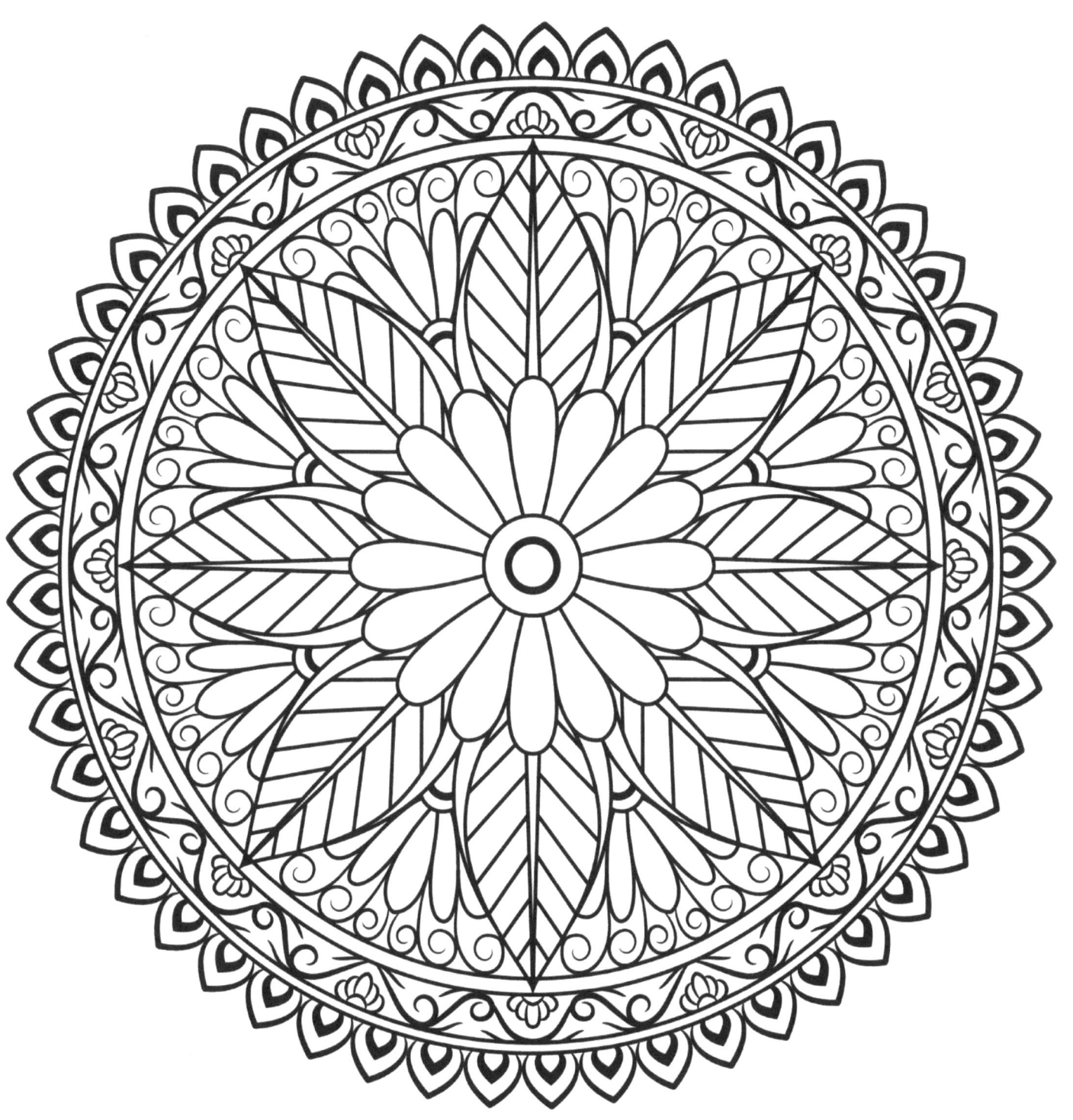

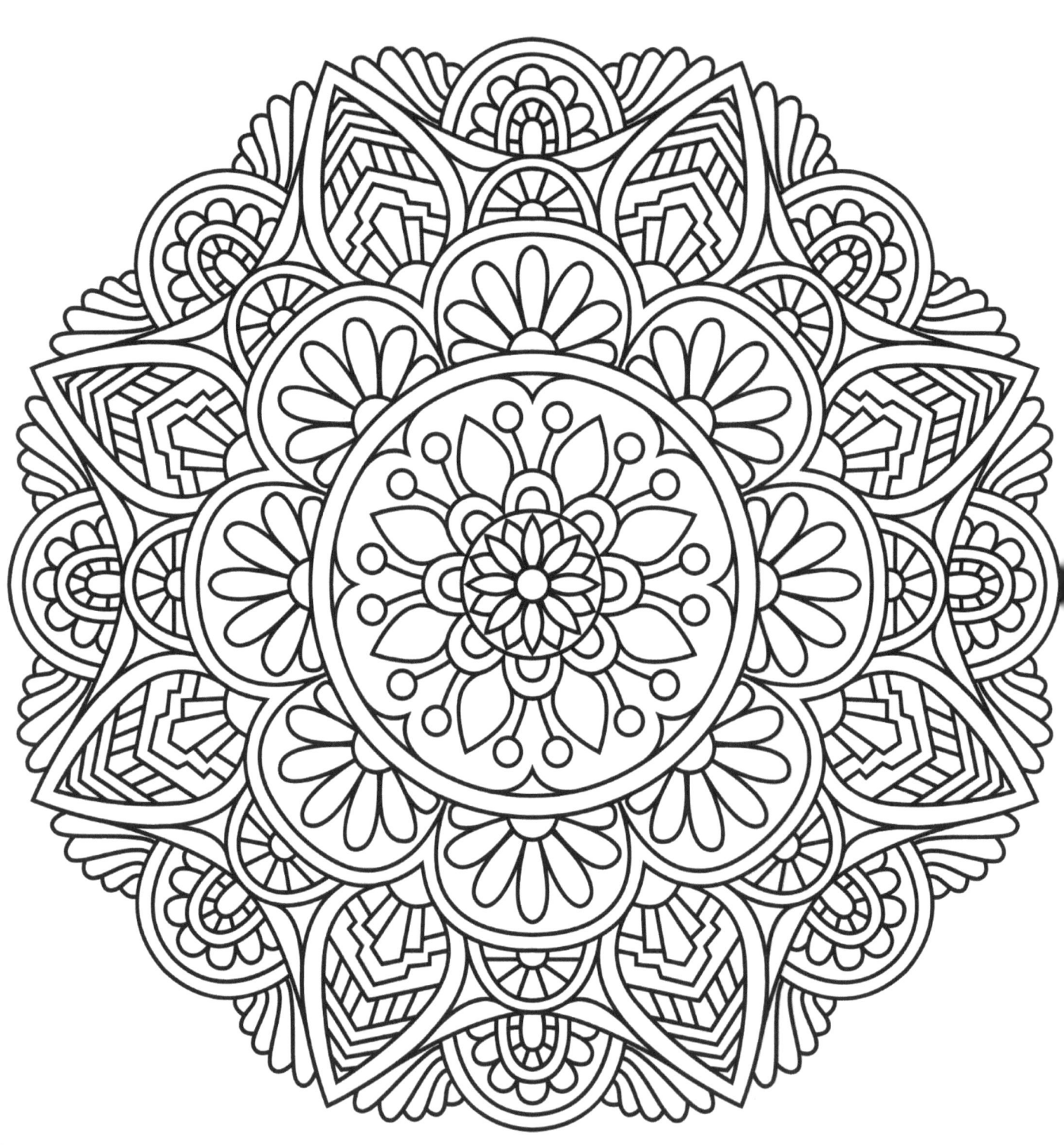

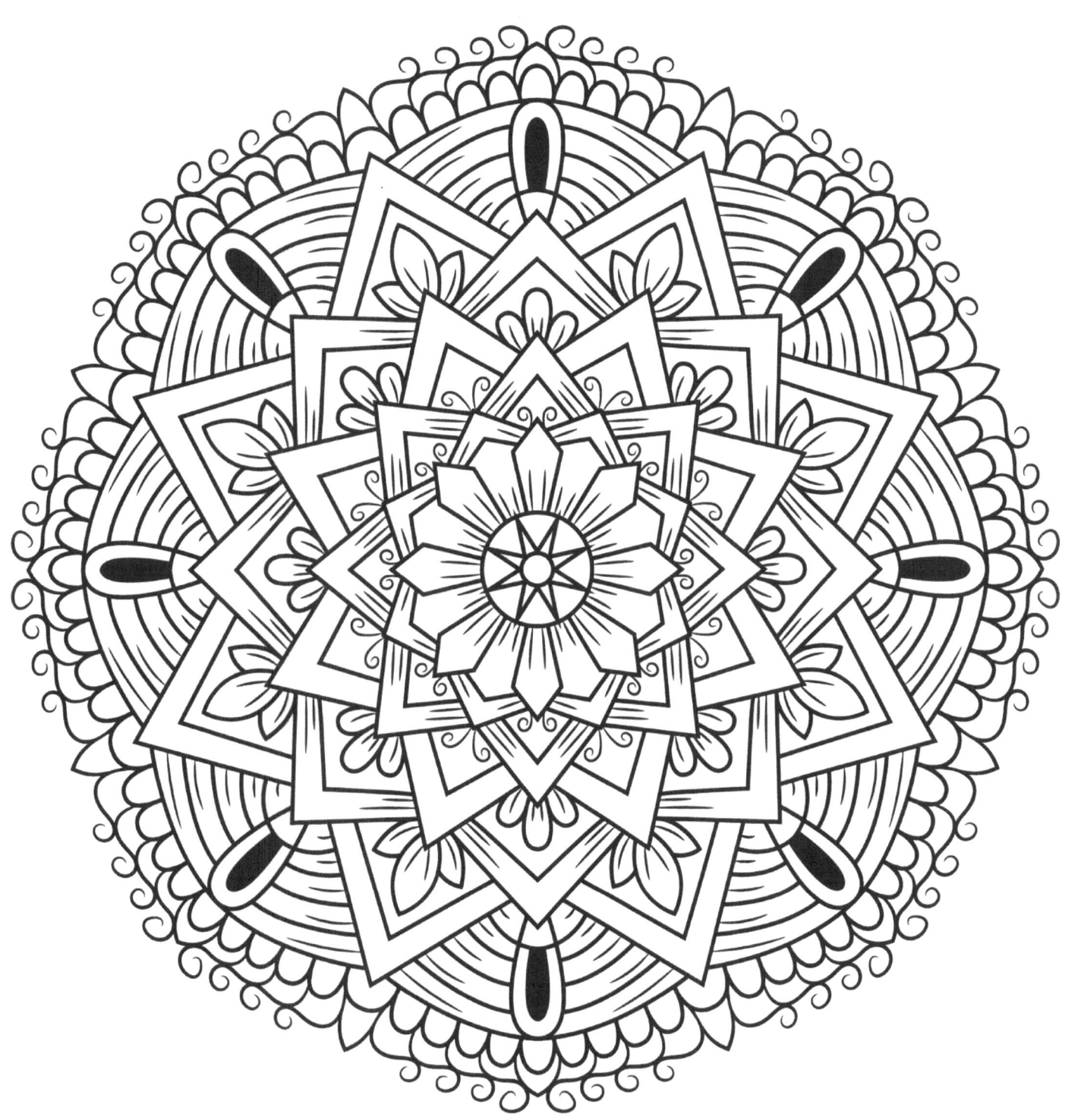

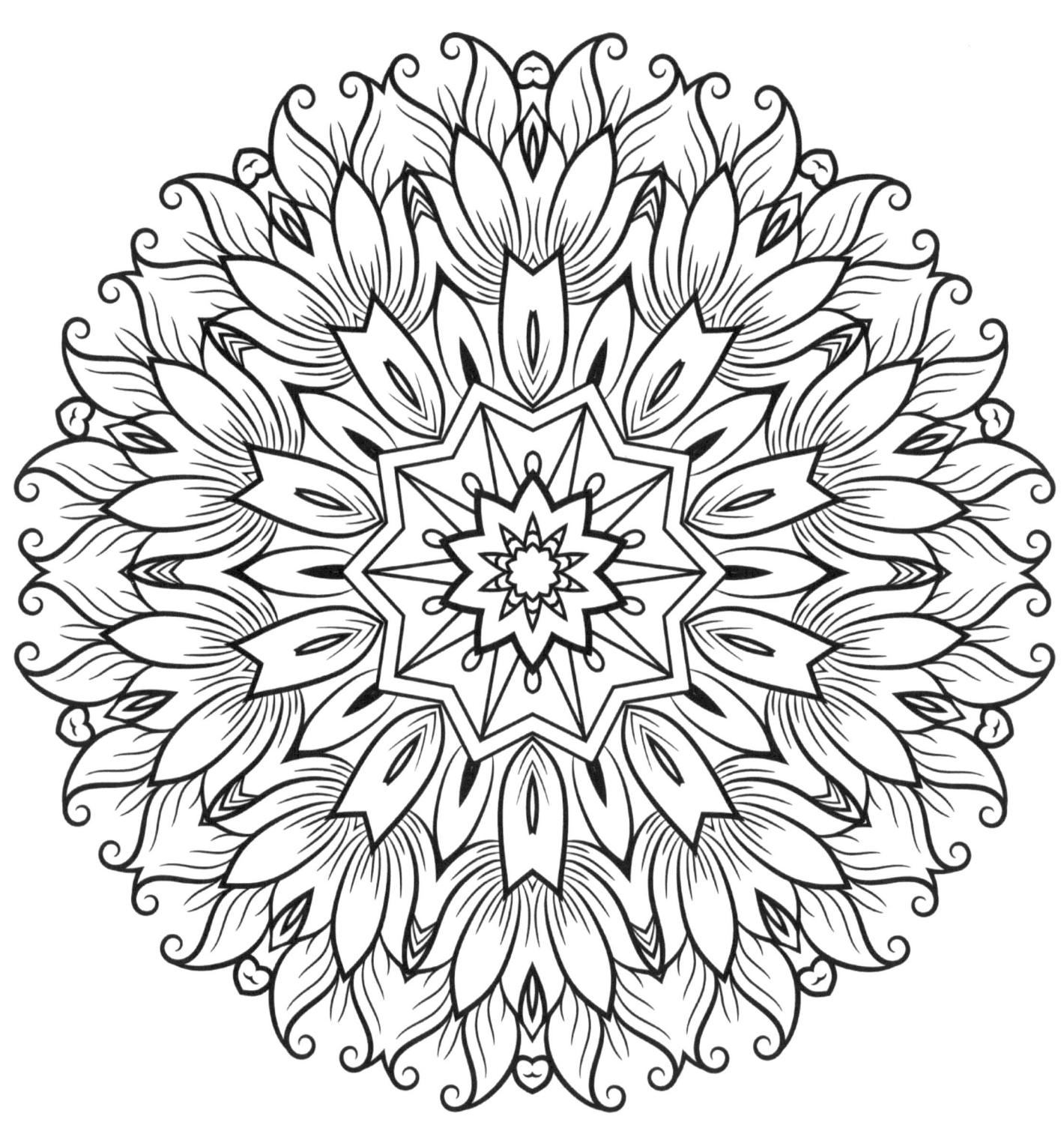

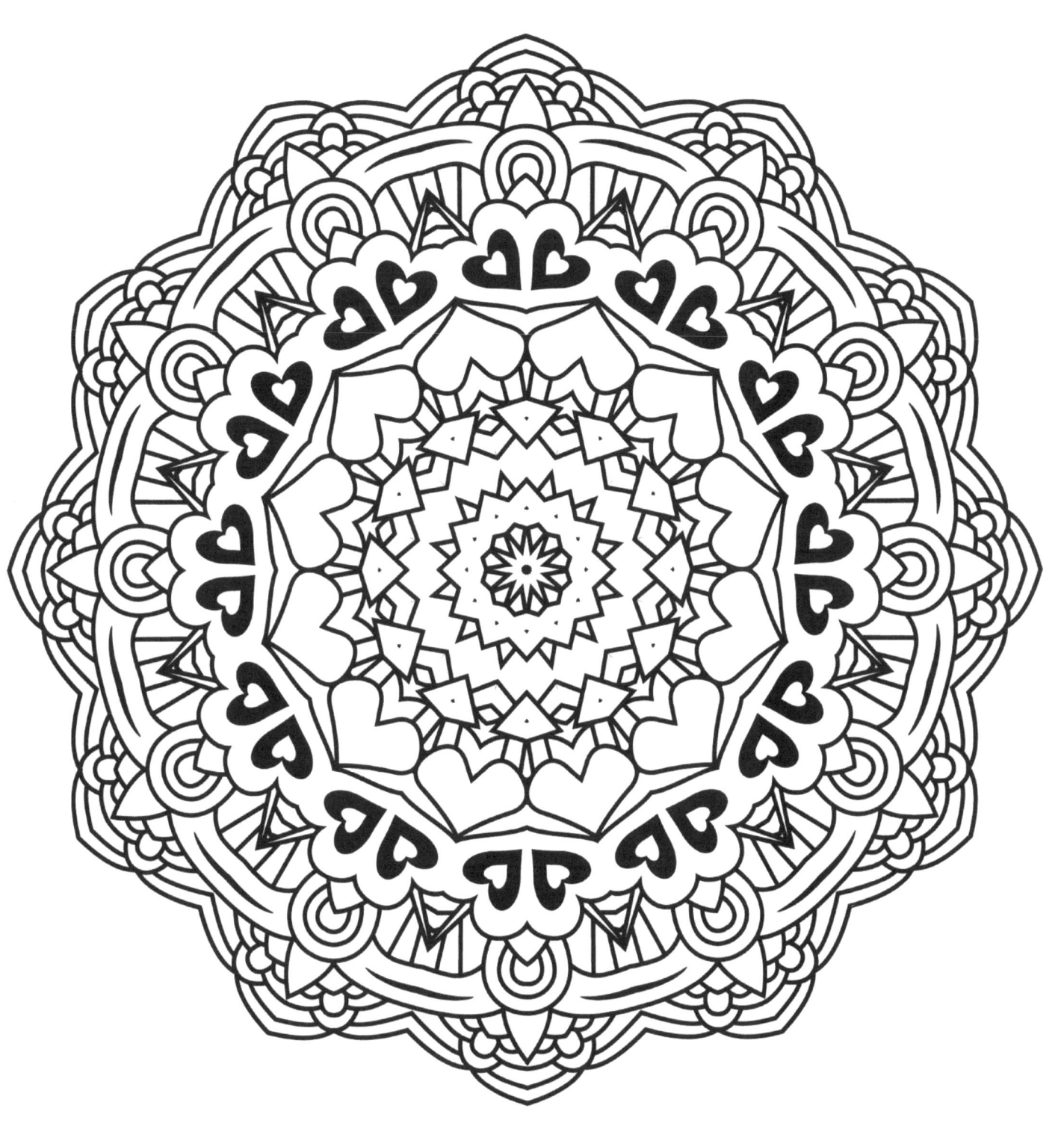

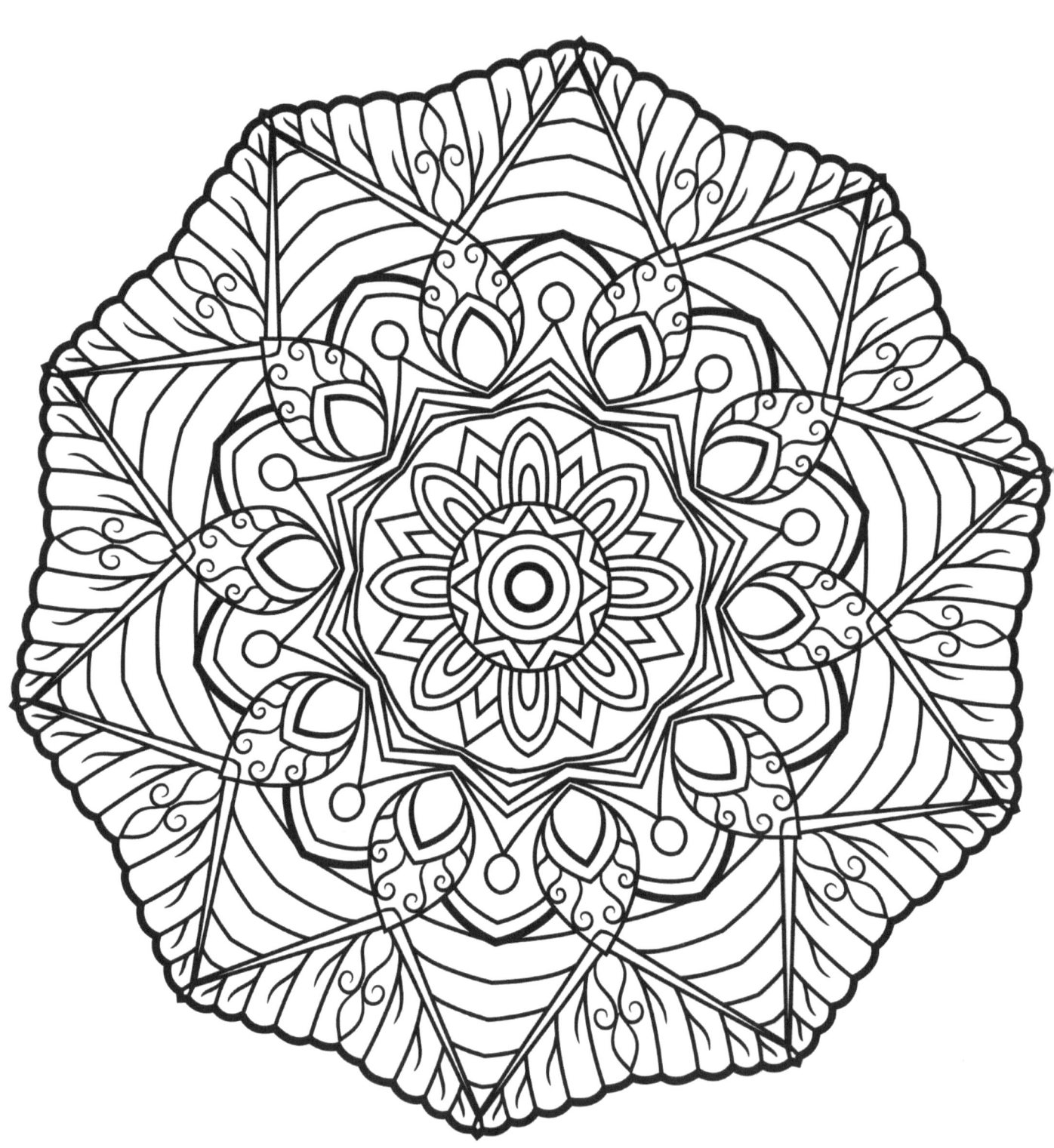

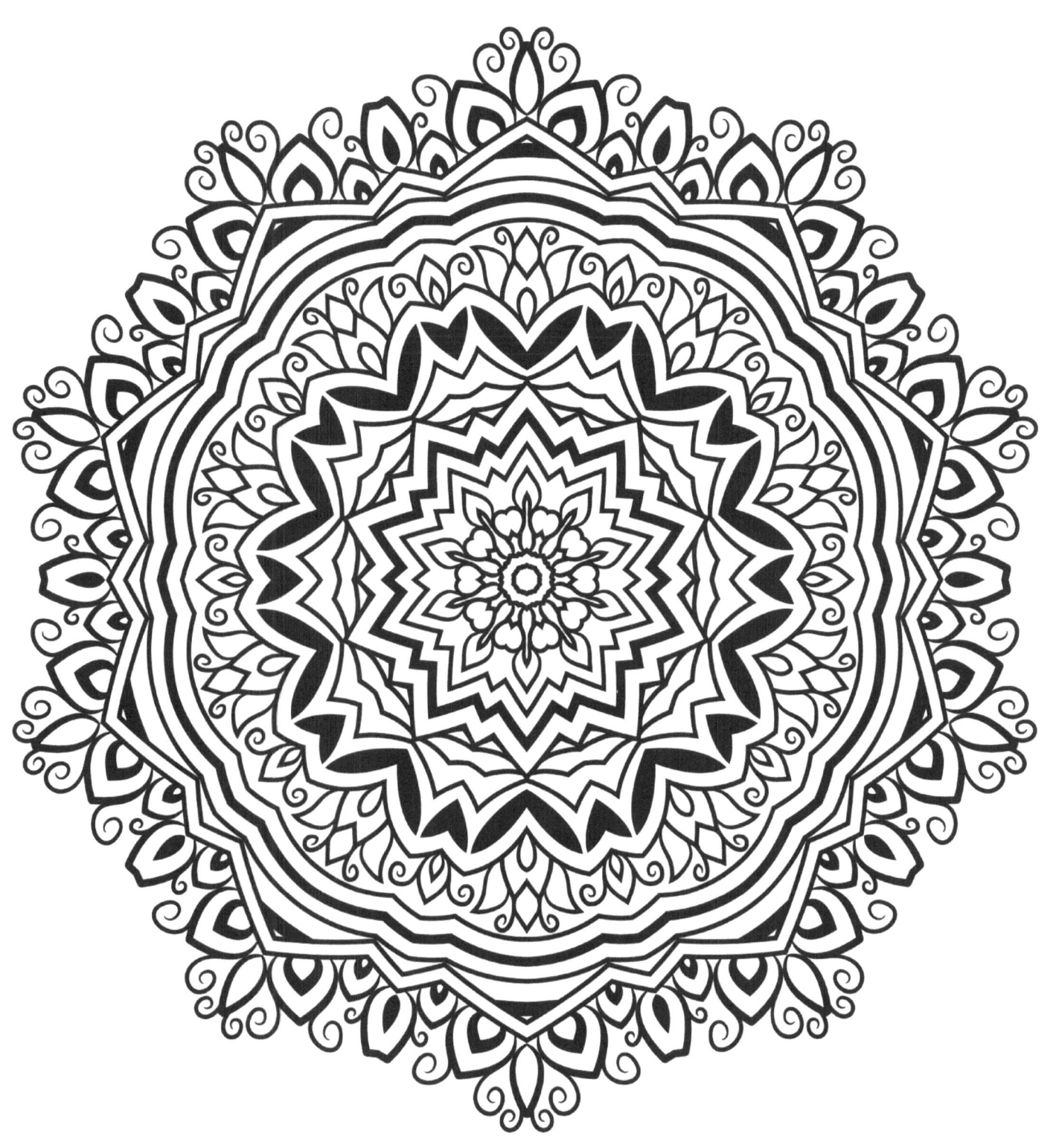

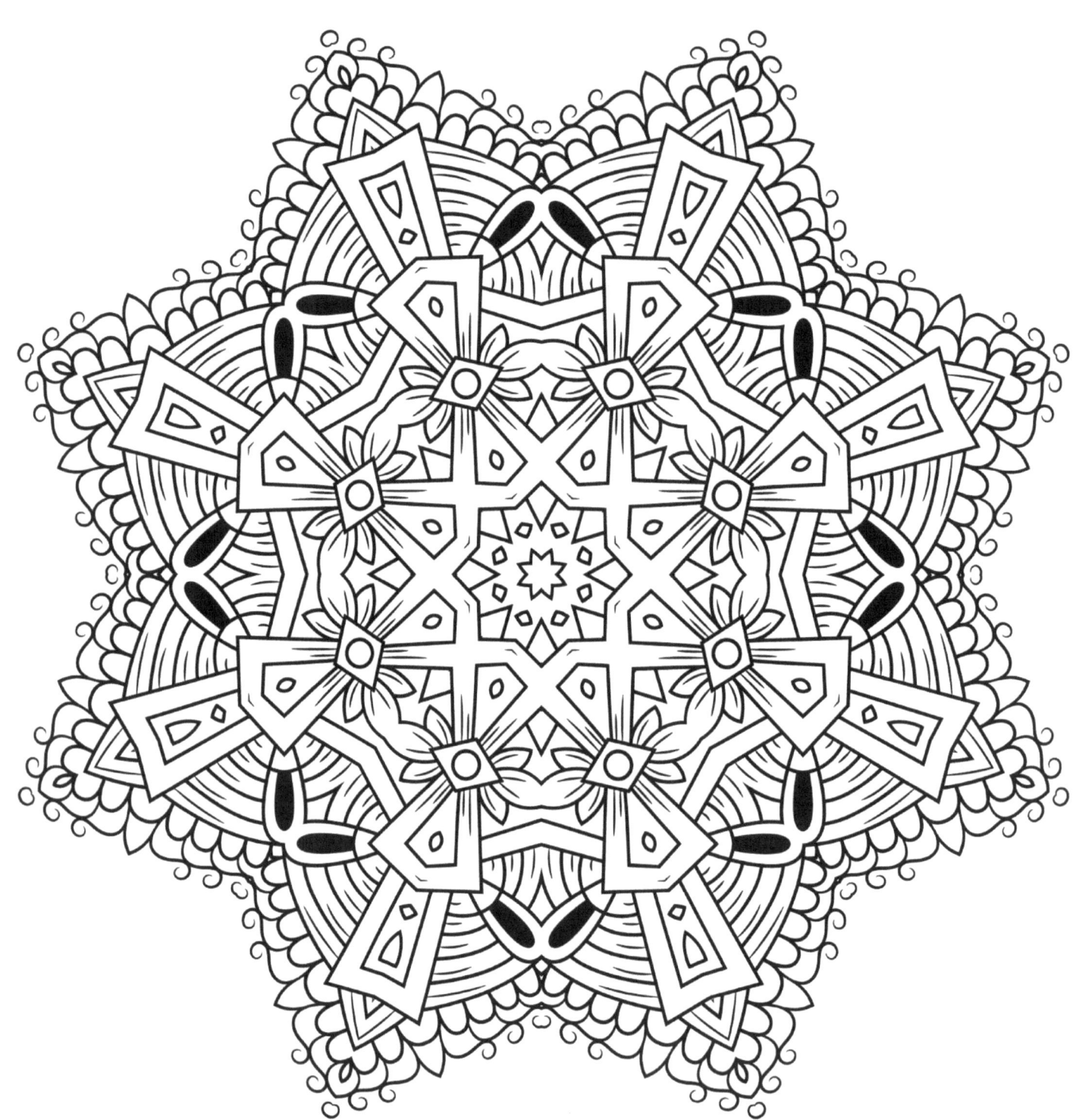

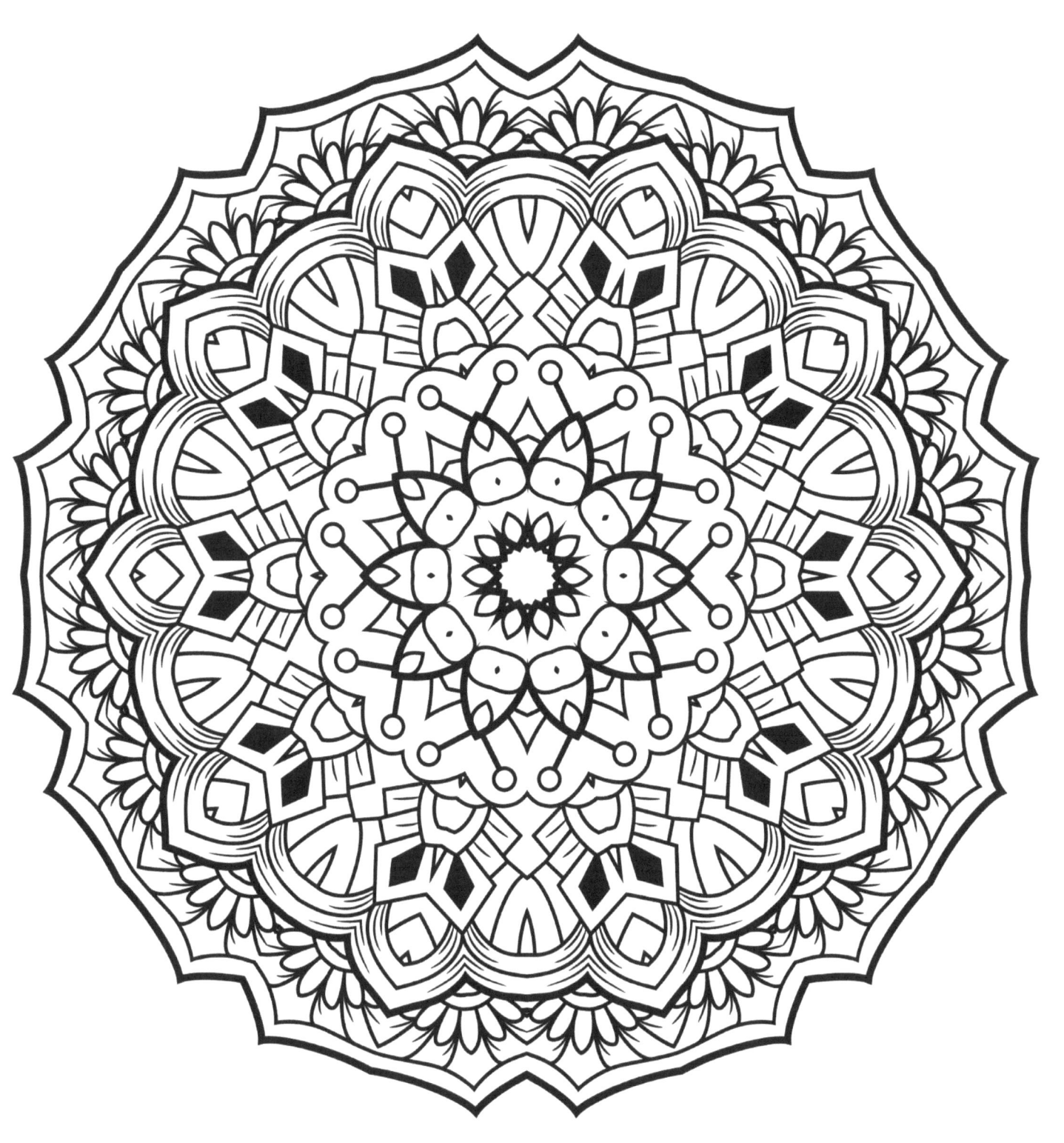

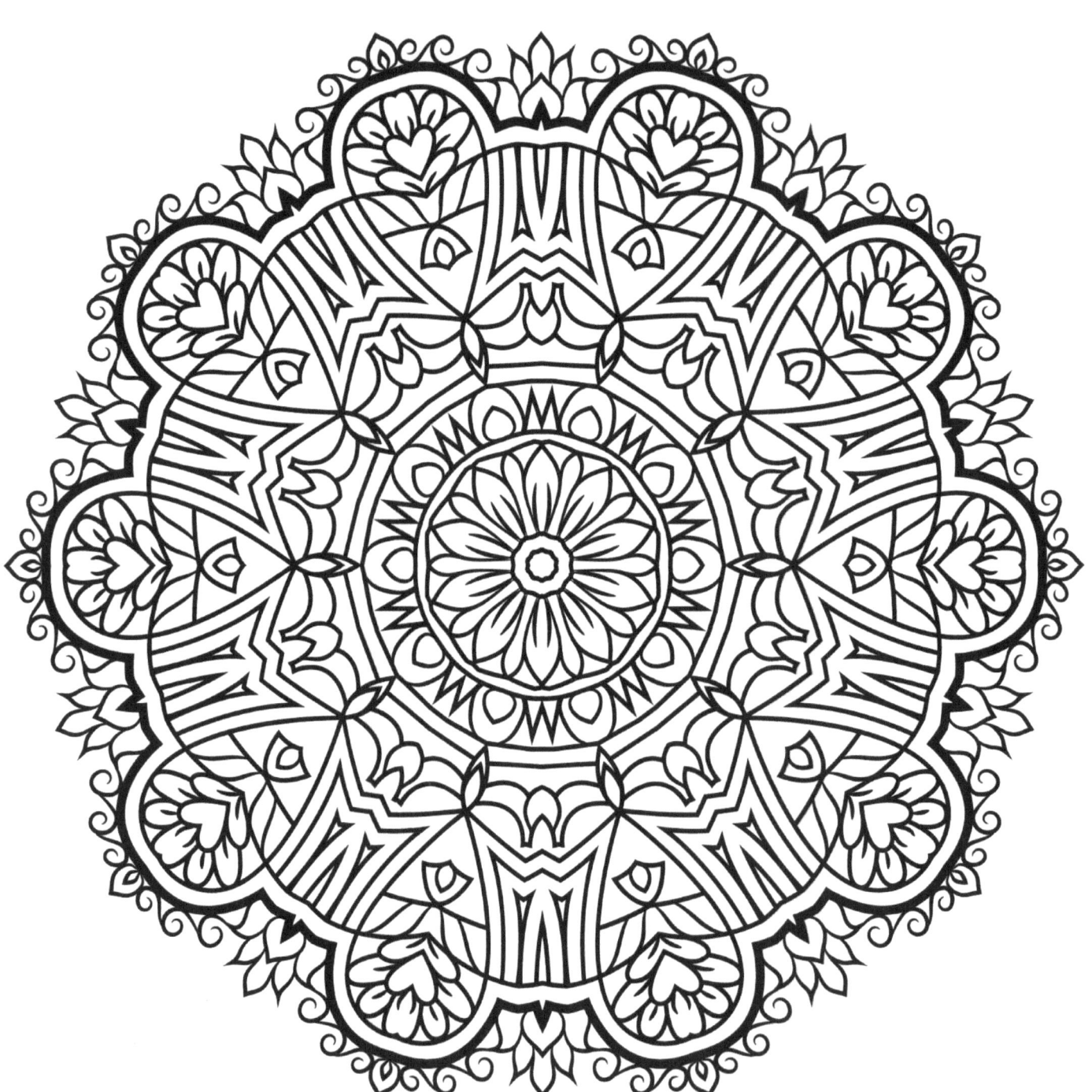

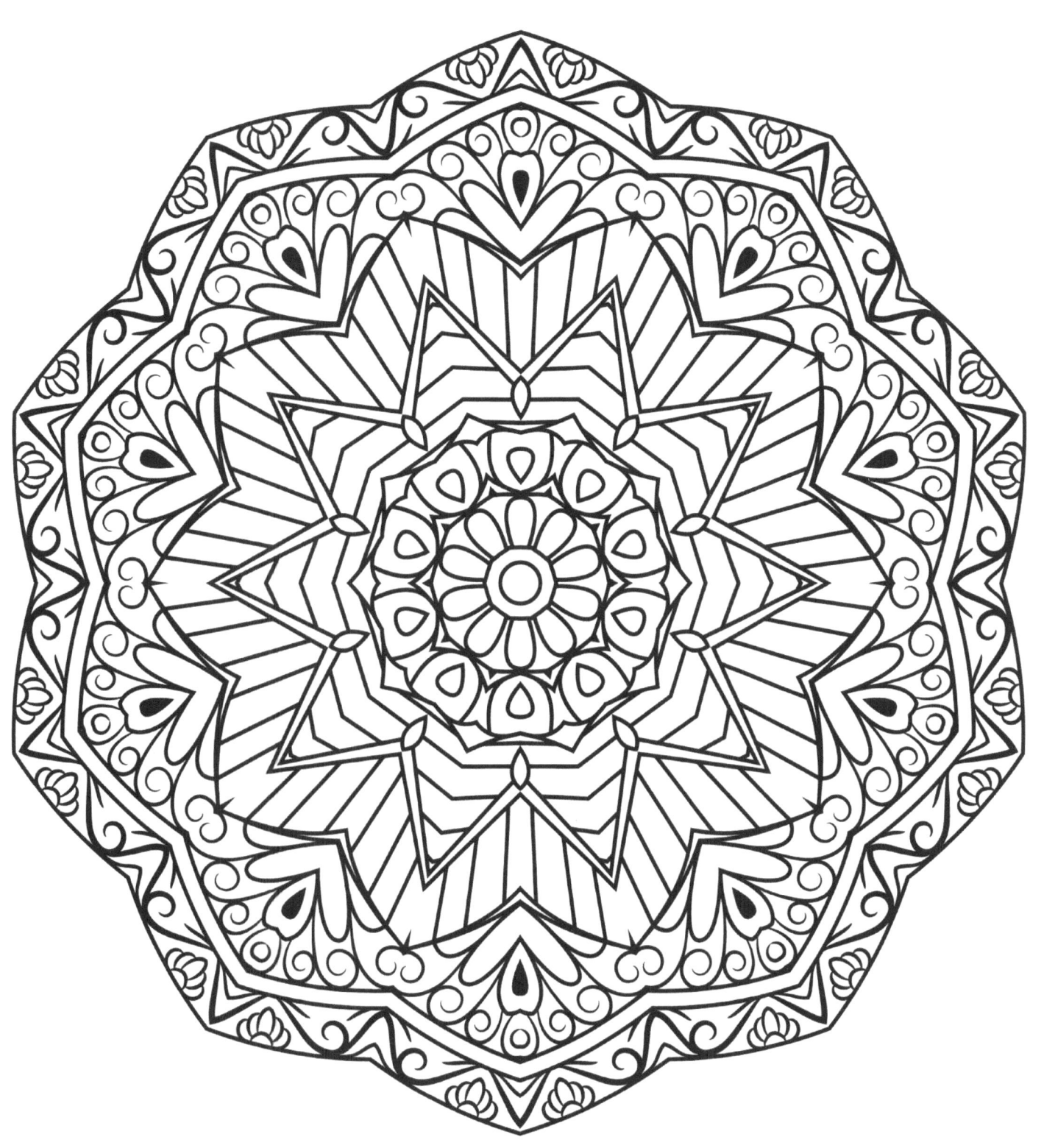

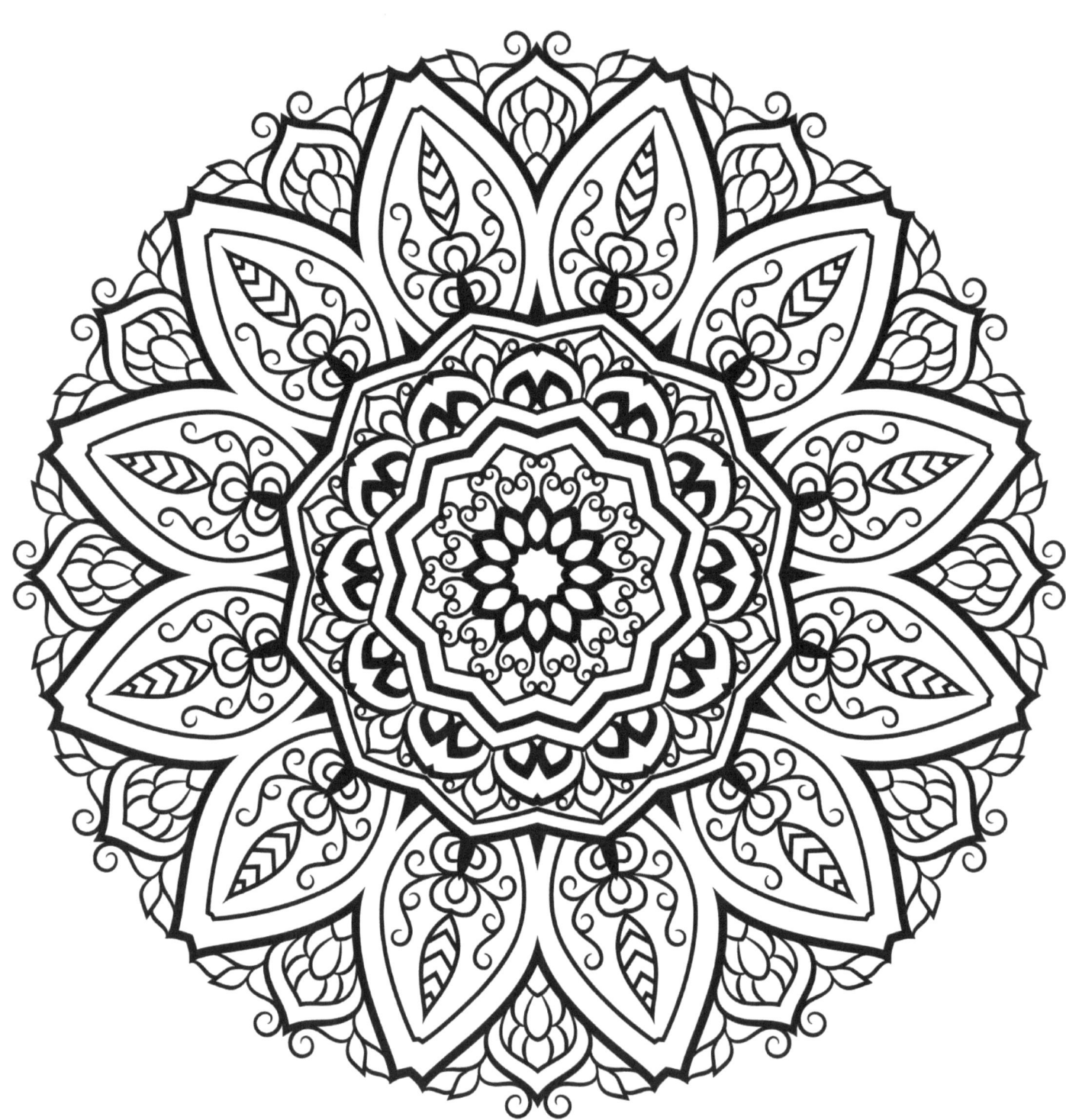

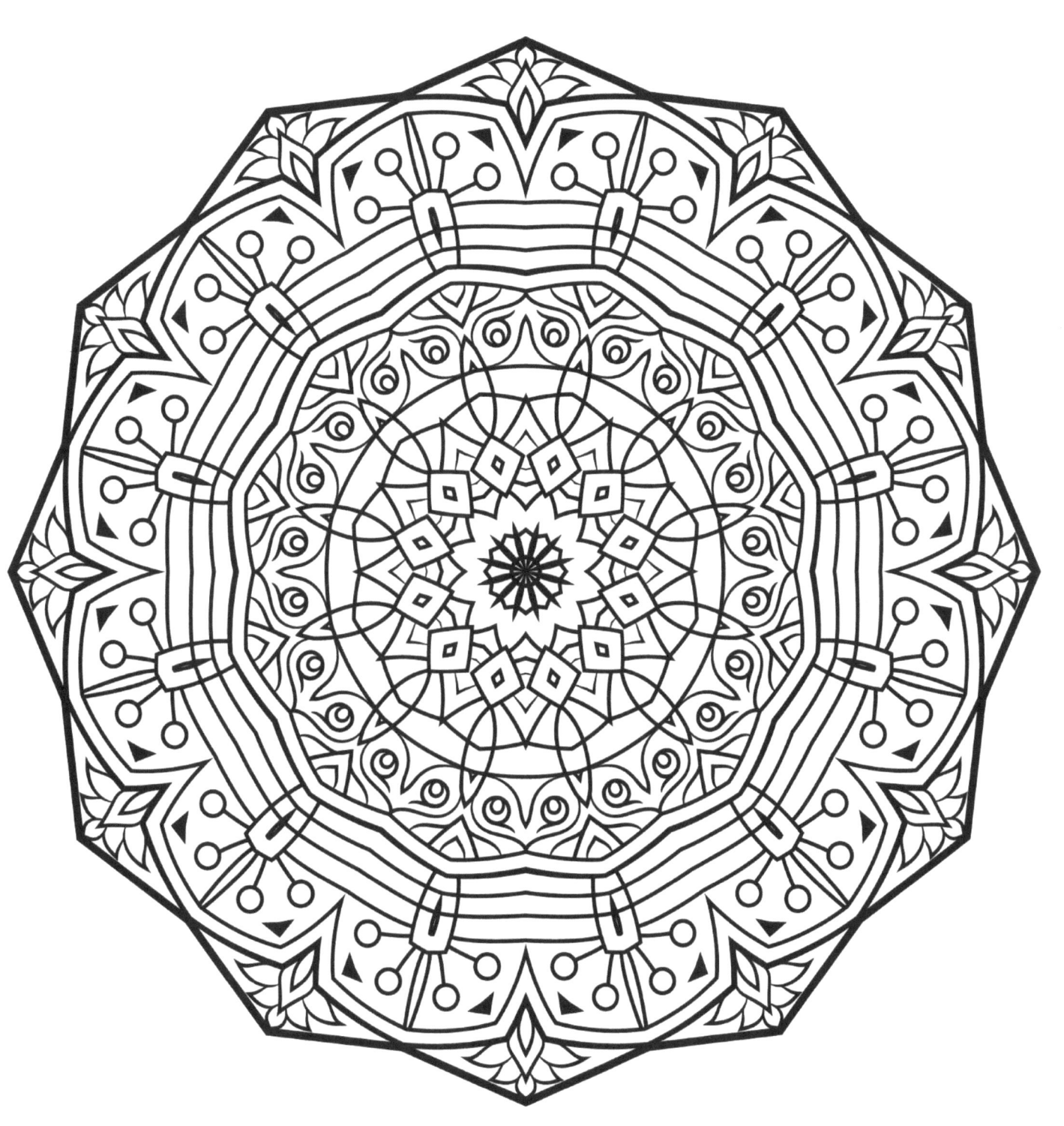

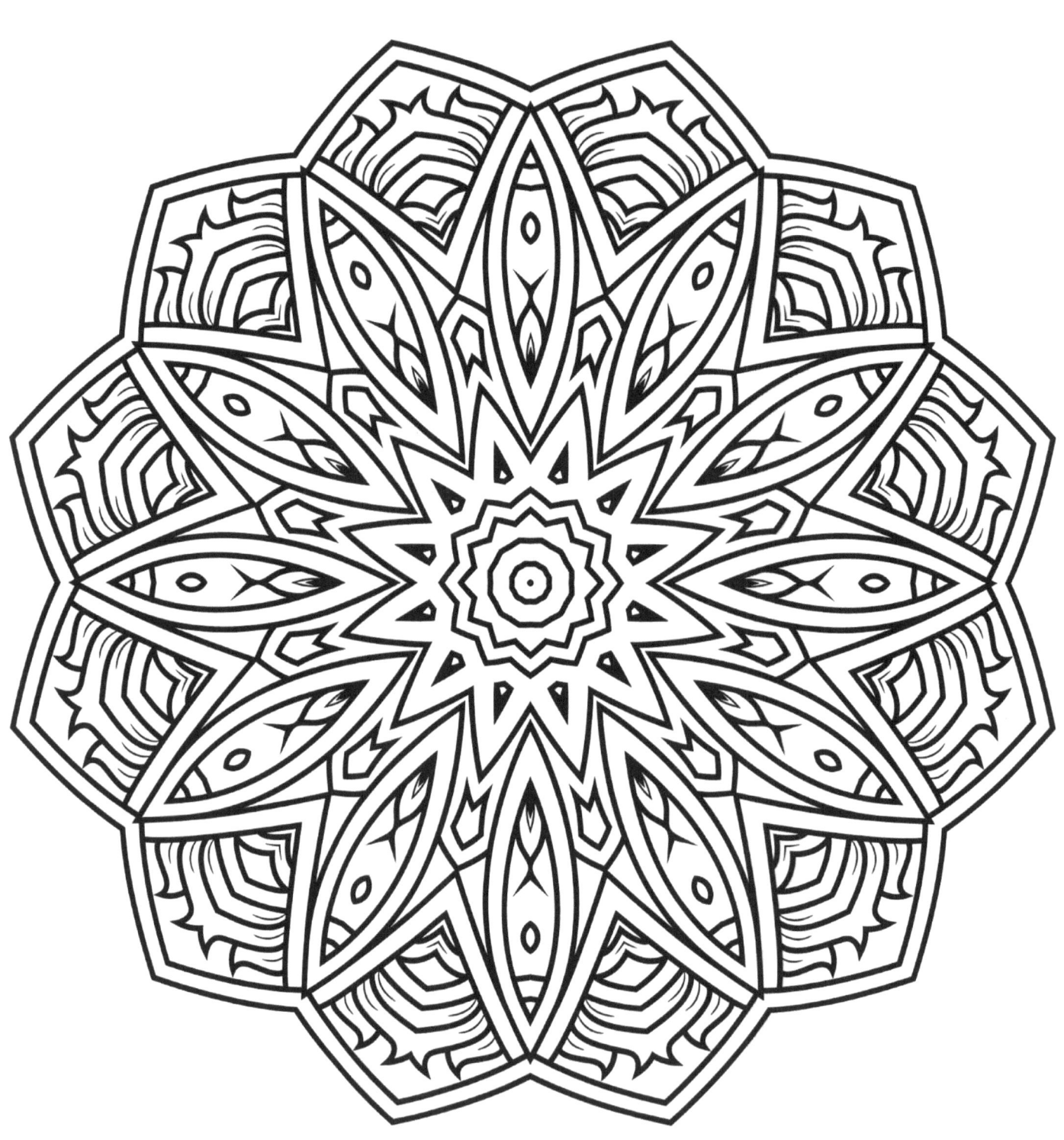

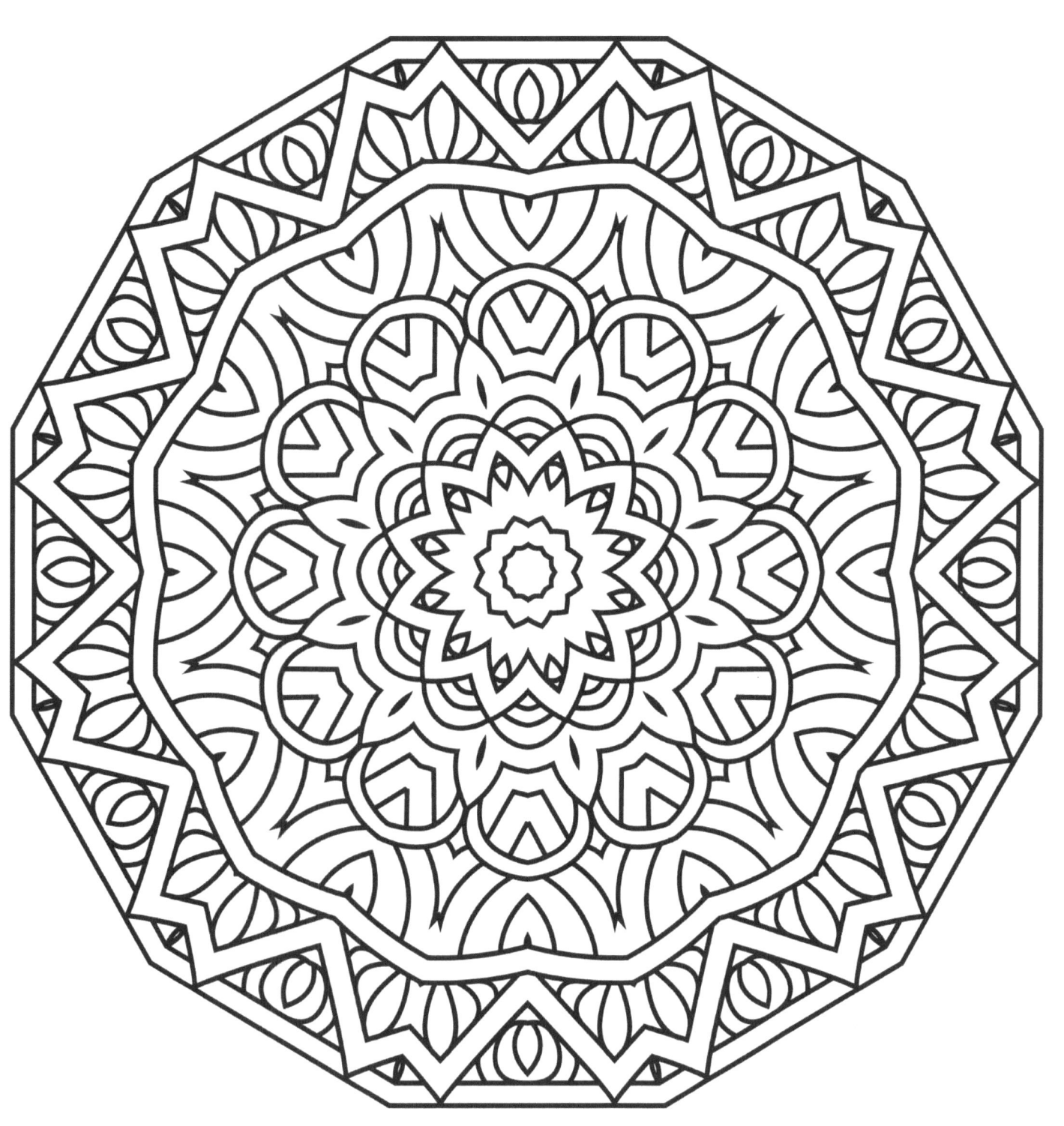

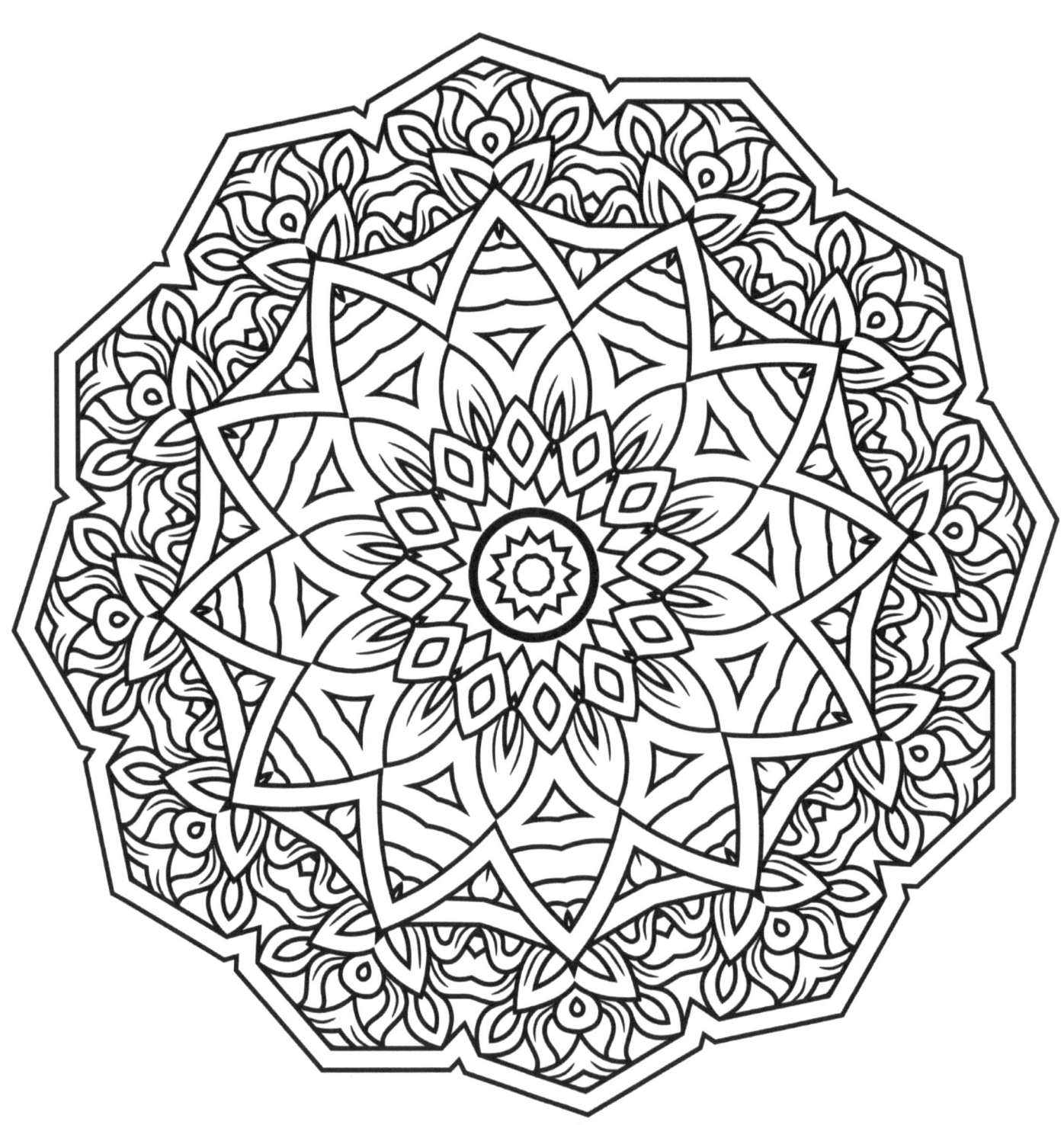

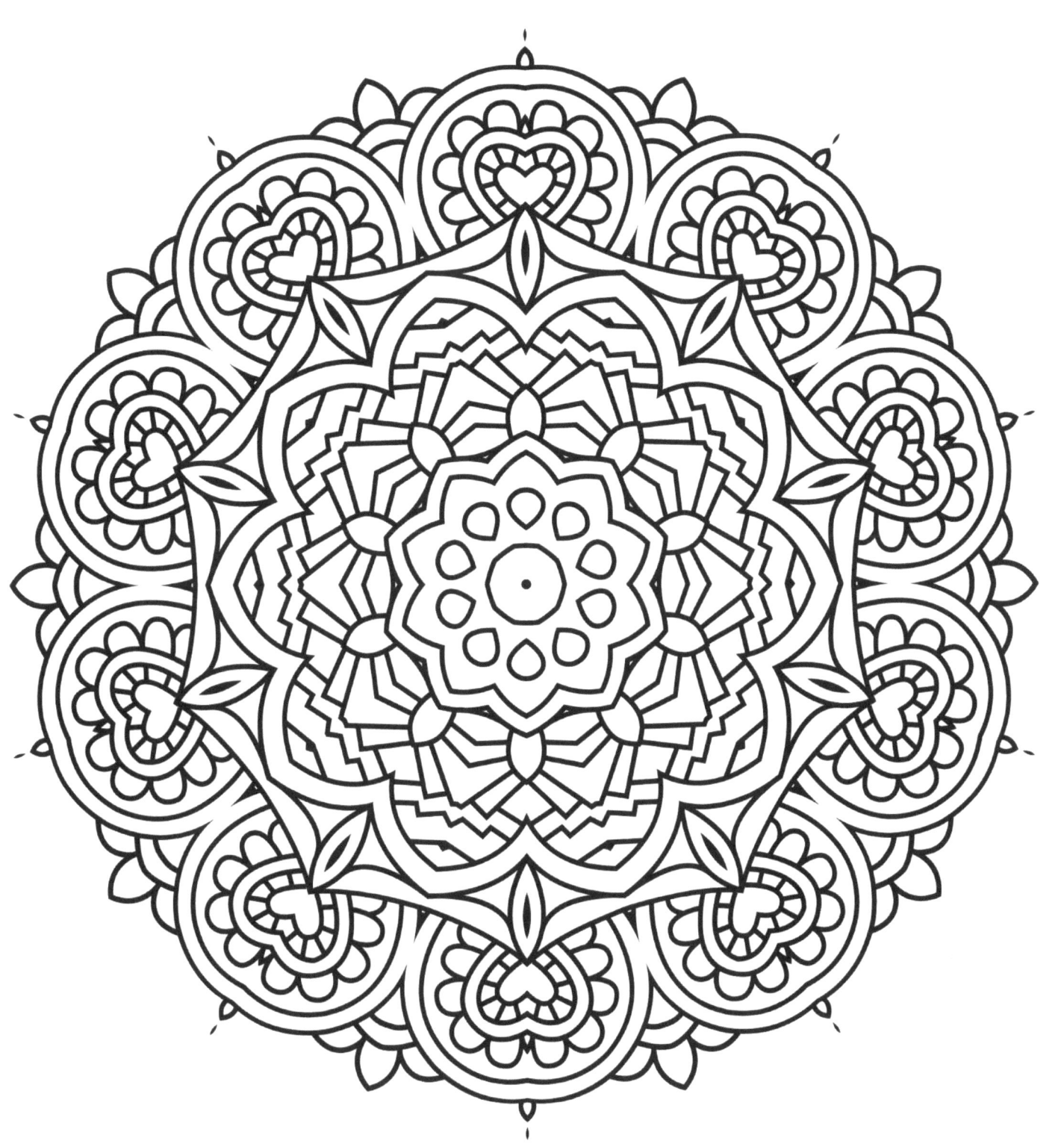

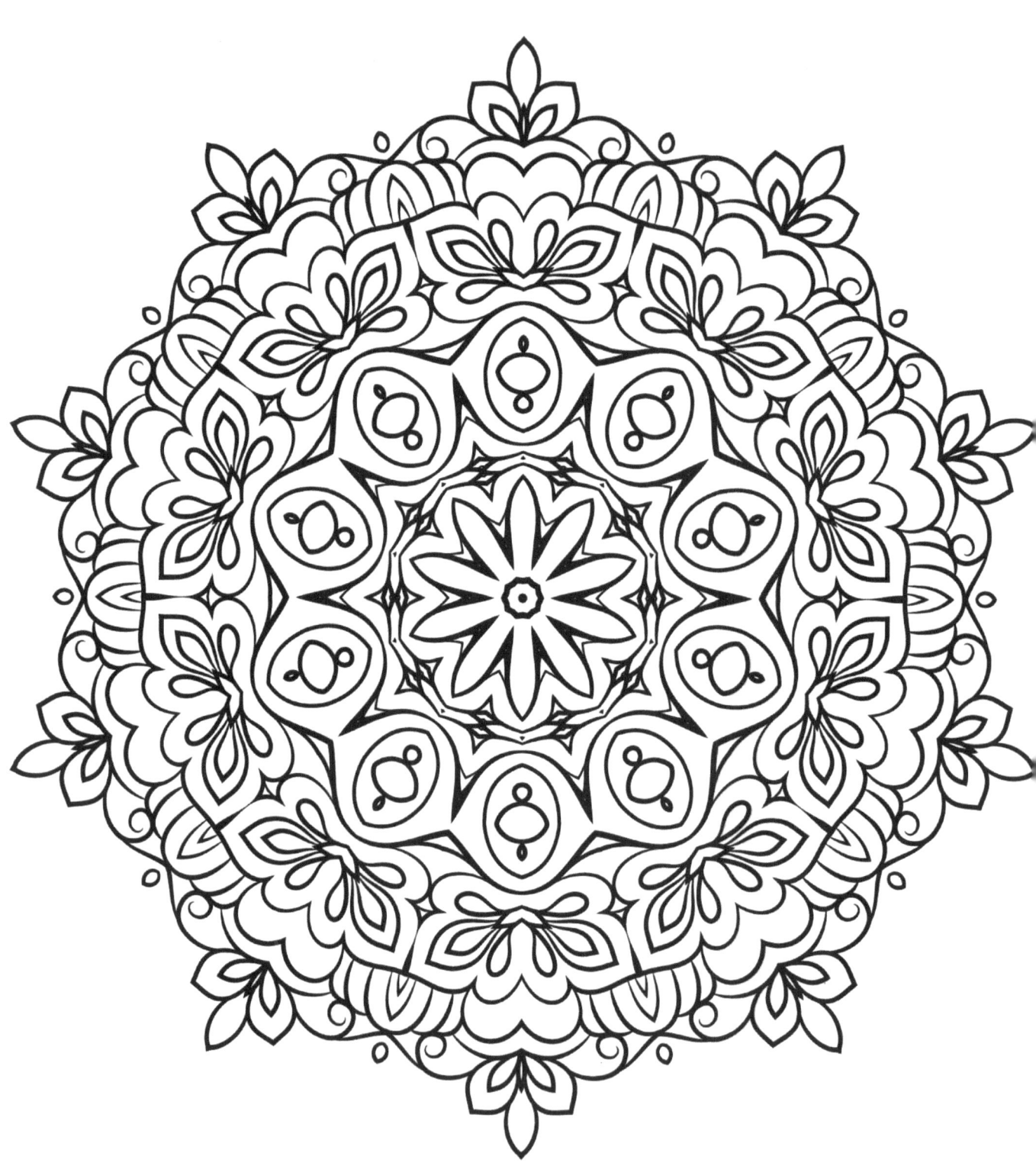